ANNE,+ ELIZABETH 08/11/2019

THANK YOU FOR SUPPORTING
DISADVANTAGED CHILDREN
THROUGH EDUCATION.

LOVE YOUR
OBSTACLES

HOW TO TURN ANY OBSTACLE INTO AN OPPORTUNITY

LOVE YOUR OBSTACLES

HOW TO TURN ANY OBSTACLE INTO AN OPPORTUNITY

SARIFA ALONTO-YOUNES

First published in 2019 by Dean Publishing
PO Box 119
Mt. Macedon, Victoria, 3441
Australia
deanpublishing.com

Cataloguing-in-Publication Data
National Library of Australia
Title: Love Your Obstacles – How to turn any obstacle into an opportunity
Edition: 1st edn
ISBN: 978-1-9254521-5-0
Category: Personal growth

DEDICATION

To the loving memories of my parents who may not have witnessed my pains, failures and the fruit of their success and achievement but whom I carried in my heart and soul every day. I will continue to keep your loving memories alive by serving humanity as long as I live.

To late Bapa Hadji Ali and late Babu Hadja Naima and late mommy Cobralin for their love and guidance. You will always be remembered in my prayers. I know you would have been very happy and proud of me if you were alive.

Also, I dedicate this book to my loving, caring and supportive husband, Hassan.

Your unconditional love, care and support continuously inspires and empowers me to do what I'm passionate to do. Your immeasurable loyalty and understanding has encouraged me to fulfil and achieve our dreams. You never hold me back from what I desire in life and your endless love and patience gives me strength to carry on and keep going.

To our dear children, Adam, Nahda, Ahmad and Dania.

I wrote this book for all of you to understand and have a glimpse of how I lived my life from a very young age and how I overcame obstacles which defined, strengthened and made me who I am today. I want you to remember that life is beautiful and meaningful when you make a difference to humanity.

CONTENTS

CHAPTER ONE

THE DARKNESS AND THE DAWN

Most three year olds think of playing with their toys or being with their siblings and parents. When I was three, I did the same. Until one day, that innocent and playful three-year-old got a glimpse of "the real world".

I remember vividly. It was April 27, 1974 and I was playing hopscotch with my friends outside our home in the Philippines. Our home was built along the National highway of Maul Marantao and was the biggest house in our neighbourhood. It had a strong timber staircase that led right up to the house; in a way it perfectly symbolised the strong welcoming hearts of my parents — they opened their arms and doors to all our neighbours and community.

Because we lived on a main highway, my siblings and I spent many hours watching traffic, counting cars that passed as we waited for Dad to come from work.

He was a respected foreman in charge of public roads construction, building and fixing roads all over the province of Lanao Del Sur. He was assigned to many different places and would only come home after the completion of a major project.

When our family received news that he was coming home, my siblings and I would excitedly drag our chairs to the window overlooking the highway and sit for hours waiting in anticipation. He mostly arrived at sunset but we never grew tired waiting. He'd turn up with his dump truck loaded with goodies like fruit, vegetables and an assortment of groceries. We would share baskets of fruit with our neighbours and relatives.

I loved when our father was home because the house became filled with visitors and overflowed with joy and happiness. Our home became vibrantly alive and was the welcoming gateway for streams of smiling guests.

But this fateful day in April, the visitors didn't come smiling, nor did they arrive for the reasons I wanted.

That morning began normally. I woke up and went straight outside to sit on our big timber staircase, tucking my knee-length floral dress underneath me, waiting for my friends from the neighbourhood to come to play.

As usual, when they woke up, my friends would run straight to our house. It was the perfect sanctuary for games, because, like many houses in the Philippines, the house is built on stilts and the first floor is two-and-a-half meters above the ground, leaving us ample space for playing under the house. We could play there all year round as it protected us from any weather. If it was too hot, we were cool and if it was raining, we were dry. Often, we only left our play area when we were hungry or when it started to get dark.

On this particular day, I remember so well, we were playing hopscotch and we decided to change our game to hide-and-seek. Our sweet carefree giggles soon became overturned by the sound of painful crying. The cries came from inside *my* home. Neighbours and relatives began rushing inside our home, the sound of their footsteps hitting the timber stairs at rapid rates.

I dropped the game we were playing and ran with the panicked crowd. My small legs manoeuvred me swiftly through the legs and waists of the crowd until I finally broke through and began frantically searching for my parents inside the house. My sister was crying uncontrollably on the floor. My other siblings were crying and relatives were wailing.

I could not see my father. *Where's father?* I thought. Crying bodies circled him. Tears dropped. They were talking out loud saying that my father had an accident, got sick and died. I looked around in disbelief as the house kept filling up with more people. I was lost amongst the mourners.

Before I could understand the surreal scene that was occurring, my father's big family began funeral arrangements almost immediately. In our Muslim culture, we believe in an afterlife and that an individual's soul gets freed from the physical body. So funerals and burials are held quickly after death in order to free the soul from the body and before the body decays.

My father's body was taken out of the house wrapped in pristine white cotton. That was the last time I saw him. I didn't get to say goodbye. It was just like a ripping separation, being immediately torn apart from the man that I loved, respected and adored.

It was impossible to fathom that such a respected, big-built, strong, dark, tall man was lifeless. His powerful, athletic and somewhat fearsome presence was no more. *How could this be?* My young mind was restless with questions and confusion.

From that moment, loneliness and emptiness filled every corner of the house. Sadness engulfed the rooms and grief lined every wall. It was as if the house was also mourning. A huge empty bore gauged into my heart, a little girl lost.

Our home didn't feel like a home anymore. I hardly saw the happy faces of all the people that used to visit us regularly. The enthusiastic gatherings that used to happen every time Dad came home faded into mere memories. The contented, happy faces of my mum and siblings were no longer present, instead expressions of worry, confusion and inner torment etched their faces and tore at their hearts. Our warm and beautiful home that was once a haven felt like a shell of itself, its exuberance deflated and its loved-filled rooms felt empty.

In my innocence, I often thought of this empty feeling like a puzzle, that if you remove one of the puzzle pieces — the entire puzzle becomes incomplete and you just can't solve it anymore. Although I was very young, the loneliness and the sadness was deep and encompassing.

After my father's passing, my siblings slowly started to move out of the house one after the other. The house saw too many changes in too little time. Over time, my siblings grew more restless and disturbed and stopped going to school. I quickly lost that playful childhood that used to fill my days, the innocent joy of playing underneath our large home with my friends. Instead, I had to find ways to cope, to understand and navigate our new stage of life, the tragic curveball thrown on us by nature and was beyond our control.

At three years of age, I was too young to go to school but my big brother Nasroding went, and I found an ingenious way to learn through his education. Perhaps it helped me deal with the grief, but for me it was like a ray of sunshine that cut through the dark looming clouds.

Every time my brother was studying or reading books, I would sit next to him or behind him listening intently to how he pronounced words, how he read them. I tried to mimic the way he read and often he'd push me away or ask me to leave because I was often copying him out loud instead of in my head. He sometimes yelled at me and told mum that I was distracting and disturbing him.

One day, he got so upset that he challenged me to

read. He pointed to the word "said" and asked me to read it out loud.

"Said" I proudly announced. He pointed to a few more simple words and he told me that if I couldn't read those words then it would be the last time I could stand around him when he was reading.

To his surprise, I read all the words that he pointed out. Innocently, I thought he would be happy for me and that I would be allowed to sit near him when he read. But the next day when I sat next to him, he read a few pages of his book and then closed the book and asked me to leave. That was the last time I was around him when he read. But it was enough to fuel my passion for learning. The flame had been lit.

A few days later I secretly took one of Nasroding's pencils and a few paper pads and started to carefully scribe different letters and words, ones I could remember from his books. Though I didn't know the alphabet I tried to mimic the curves and lines I had seen.

One day my other brother Daud came home and saw my brother Nasroding reading his book. Daud was older and he sat next to Nasroding in order to test his reading skills. He pointed to many complicated words and asked him to pronounce them. Nasroding struggled a little bit and Daud called for my attention in order to tease Nasroding. He asked me to read knowing full well I wasn't in school yet. I took the book and opened the same page where Nasroding had struggled, Daud was trying to help me read the book believing that perhaps I'd never seen words before. He was surprised and dumbfounded when I read. Daud jumped up and down excitedly and grabbed me, "Oh my God! She is reading. She knows how to read!" he said.

He looked into my eyes and said, "How did you learn? Who taught you?"

I gazed at him speechless because I didn't know what to say. I thought it was normal; like when I played with my friends. We didn't need to be taught, we played by instinct. I never once thought that teaching myself to read and write before school was unusual.

All I knew was that I enjoyed it, I was captivated with words and learning, and that's all I needed to know.

CHAPTER TWO

THE MOMENT MY WORLD CHANGED FOREVER

Finally, the day had arrived. I was old enough to go to school. It was a proud day and one of the happiest of my young life. I had been looking forward to it and waiting with excited anticipation for that special day. I was finally a schoolgirl, and an eager one at that.

School was my second home. I felt at ease learning, it was the one area I felt truly confident. Yet, while I was busy learning and making future plans, life was busy making other future plans for me. Plans I didn't want nor was prepared to handle.

Through my early school years, my mother developed stomach cancer, a cruel and devastating disease. Every day was a battle for her. I could see her physical pain and I could feel her emotional pain inside my own heart. Her love for me was so grand that every time I asked how she was, she would simply reply "I'm fine, Sarifa."

But she wasn't fine. She didn't take any medication and some days I could see her wince in pain though she tried in vain to hide it from me. I prayed and hoped for a miracle.

She desperately tried to shelter me from her struggles and suffering but my heart knew the truth. How could I *not* see my dear mother wither and struggle? I felt her pain every time I looked at her. Tears cascaded through my heart but I made sure they never made it to my eyes in front of her. I couldn't bear the pain that I knew she was going through.

One day, in grade four, I made a decision to not attend school the next day. Though I loved school, I had a deep, strong feeling that the next day would be her last day. I couldn't sleep that night, tossing and turning with an ache in my soul.

In the morning, I prepared myself psychologically and emotionally. I knew in my heart that she was going to pass away. That I wouldn't see her again. That my life would change forever.

I remember sitting next to her bed with my grandmother. I looked at my mother and reached to touch her. She was cold but she looked normal. The pain that usually tormented her was absent this particular day. It was the only minor relief in a day of brutal hardship.

While she was laying down, I was trying to make conversation with her in case she had an important message to say before she went. Since she was not in pain, I insisted to my grandmother that I would cut my mother's fingernails and her toenails, and then give her a sponge bath. I wanted to take care of her, to love and nurture her one last time. She looked so beautiful as I tenderly trimmed her nails and washed her gently, sponging her sweetly and hoping she could feel the love pouring through me.

Clean and warm, my mother rested, her pain still unusually absent. I was overcome with love for her. I couldn't stop planting cherished kisses all over her. My entire being was overwhelmed with pure love yet I was simultaneously aching in deep anguish as the inevitable moment approached.

My endless kissing and conversation not only revealed my deep adoration and devotion to her, but in some mysterious way I could feel her surrounding me with the same silent beauty. She knew the pain I had in letting her go yet I also didn't want to see her suffer. I was not ready to live without her, I didn't know if I could and yet I didn't want her to live like this.

In a serendipitous moment, mum reached for me and we clutched our hands together. Her familiar deep brown eyes looked straight into mine and she squished my hand; a delicate teardrop in the shape of a small pearl sat perfectly on her cheek as she closed her eyes one last time. Her hand rested in mine but her final signal, that loving squish of my hand still pulsated through me.

My grandmother quickly asked me to get a glass of water from the kitchen. I didn't know at the time that she was trying to protect me from what had just happened. When I returned, grandmother was looking over my mother crying, grandmother reached for me and pulled me into a tight warm hug. I placed the water down and shut my eyes tightly. We cried together. My mother was gone. I knew deep down that we'd taken a unique journey together. That as we held hands, she had entered a new life and so had I.

Part of me did not want to disturb her soul's journey because I knew that she had suffered enough. And yet, the child within me only wanted her to stay. My inner cries pleaded for her to stay with me, to watch me grow. To love me and for me to love her. Forever.

I prayed for strength, for God to help me. I had never been more lost. I didn't want to take this journey alone.

At ten years of age, my fate was sealed. I was an orphan.

Life would never be the same. I had to grow and learn to cope emotionally.

My aunt and cousin's family took me in and treated me like their daughter and sister, showering me with love and affection together with her other seven children. Though I was the eldest amongst them and was surrounded by love, I missed my parents so much that I was losing a sense of direction. Confusion was taking over me and I didn't know how to stop it.

The vortex of hurt and confusion filled my heart and I spent many sleepless nights crying under my pillow longing for their love. I spent long lonely nights praying and hoping to see them in my dreams. I missed them terribly and sought comfort from them in any possible way — even if I only had dreams and memories for solace.

I felt lost and alone and like no one really knew or understood what I was going through. I ached inside. The times I got sick, I cried even more. Not because I was sick but because I wished that my mother would be there for me. I longed for her hugs, love and maternal comfort. She was the only medicine that I was truly seeking and I felt that even one tender hug would be enough to heal me, to cure me for life.

I tried to talk to myself, to search, to find some understanding and strength inside. I needed to know how to get out of misery. I needed to discover it soon before the heavy blanket of misery suffocated me.

I felt that I had lost everything. My parents were my everything. Losing one was hard, losing two was unbearable.

What would life possibly hold for me now? At ten years old I felt that the worst had happened. My parents had died. They would never be here to see me grow up, to help me grow up, to be proud of my achievements or share in a simple family gathering. Emptiness and insecurity knocked at the door of my soul every day. Would I be strong enough to push it away?

I soon learnt that when in grief, many people's well-meaning words fall short. Not because they aren't filled with support and love, they certainly are, but because they can't fill that deeper void within.

No matter how hard people tried to offer me solace

and comfort through their kind words — I didn't find my way out of misery that way. But one sentence did circle my mind like a longing seed floating in the wind seeking a warm place to germinate and grow.

Words my mother had said played over and over in my head. "Education will drag you out of misery. If you want to succeed, you need to understand the power of education." The sweet remembrance of her guiding voice flooded my consciousness.

Six-months after the death of my mother something transformative dawned on me. I realised that I had the power within me to accept my circumstances, and in doing so, I was able to control how I was feeling and thinking. Learning to accept would help me stop fighting and resisting what had already happened. When I began to accept the harsh fact that my parents were no longer there for me, it somehow eased my pain and suffering. It soothed the wound little by little.

This was a huge turning point for me. Though the world still looked rather bleak to me in terms of assessing the scope of my future, I did understand that the path was right in front of me, in fact, I was standing right on the path. That path was education. I could now walk forward.

Accepting the obstacle of being an orphan allowed me to move forward, concentrate on my studies and continue my education. Without parents to comfort me, I decided that study would be my safety blanket and school would be considered a home.

I decided to do well at school. I aimed higher,

to achieve, to learn faster and better than before. I understood that scholarships were based on performance and I wanted to reach beyond what I could see locally. I began imagining a life beyond my hometown and local educational institution. That was my inner 'why' — my golden ticket out of misery. This was the fuel that ignited my drive every day, to do not only my best, but to do my very best in everything.

My drive became fierce. Relentless. When I returned home after school, I helped do chores inside the house. And when I was at school, I ensured that I listened attentively to the teacher. I would not miss one second of learning. I would memorise and write down the exact words the teacher said because I thought that was the art or the secret to success. I didn't want to miss out on anything. I went to school regardless of the weather or my health. It was a purpose-driven quest.

I trained myself to become very, very attentive inside the classroom so I didn't miss out on a single piece of critical information. And then, in exams, this became my 'secret weapon'. I could tap into all the information reserves that were stored in my memory through attentive listening and note-taking. I made it my inner duty to come first in exams and I graduated grade six as a Valedictorian.

Life had shown me that anything could happen. That life could be short and unpredictable. I didn't know the higher answers to my circumstances but I did know one thing. The one thing that my mother had said — that I needed to study hard, because only education would drag me out of misery. I clung to this possibility like it was my last breath.

That one sentence filled me with hope and gave me a reason to live, to believe that I had a purpose and could one day make a difference. I wasn't good at anything else except studying. So my road was narrow but education was my ticket. I'd take the narrow road because it was also the only one I had. A one-way ticket was all I would need.

Fuelled with this burning ambition, I received more recognition from teachers and earned scholarships that allowed me to advance in school and on to higher education. I excelled at everything I put my mind to. It was hard work and took a tremendous amount of commitment and dedication; at one point it looked like I was not going to be considered for a scholarship that I'd tried my heart out for, it nearly shattered my hopes. But I couldn't give up. I couldn't give up on my dreams.

Finally, after a lot of blood, sweat and tears, I managed to receive a scholarship during my high school period. Later, I passed the university scholarship exam at Mindanao State University. This helped me receive a scholarship at the International Islamic University (IIUM) in Kuala Lumpur, Malaysia where I obtained both a Bachelor and Masters Degree in Psychology.

Being in an international university meant that my contemporaries were from all over the world and the breadth of this peer group allowed me to set my goals higher and higher. I was invited to attend events and present at universities in Europe, Asia, Middle East and back home in the Philippines.

It also meant that I was alone again in the world, but this time I was going somewhere. It was a doorway to my future life journey.

I got involved in leadership; educational, social, environmental issues and campaigns, and other projects that led me to either organise or participate in various conferences and seminars both nationally and internationally. I often spoke on behalf of our student groups and university organisations addressing academia, media and even political leaders.

It didn't take me long to realise that I had far greater opportunities open to me than simply returning to my hometown in Marawi City, Philippines with degrees in my hand. Life had changed and so had my ideas of what was possible. Not only did my education pull me out of my hopeless situation but it also gave me the life-changing opportunity to meet the man that would later become my husband, Hassan.

Our love was built on the foundation of understanding and we broadened our horizons together by getting married and moving to Melbourne, Australia in 1998. We were from different cultures too and this inevitably came with its own set of obstacles to overcome.

Over time, I was able to earn my second Masters Degree in Education and Training at the University of Victoria, Melbourne, Australia.

Now, I hold both masters in Industrial and Organizational Psychology and Education and Training.

With years gone by, looking back in reflection, I can now see that the obstacle of being an orphan did not break me, rather it defined and strengthened me beyond my wildest imagination.

These days, as I tour the country speaking to thousands of people, I have come to see that we all have struggles, that we all want to try and ease suffering and create a life that we love. And my dream is to help other people do this too. This is my new dream.

I would like to share my pathway to success with you. Though your struggles may be different to mine, I have discovered that certain teachings are universal and they work on a broad spectrum of problems.

I will hold your hand along the way. I will support your journey and your dreams and try to shed some light into how you can truly see your obstacles as opportunities.

This book isn't just to read, it's to use as a tool, it's here to help you achieve your dreams.

Throughout the book there are various pages for notes, they are to encourage you forward in life. To accept. To decide. To dream. To plan your life full of possibility.

"A tree with strong roots laughs at storms."
Malay Proverb

CHAPTER THREE

THE PROMISE AND THE PATHWAY

Before I shed more light on my journey, I want to look at why it's often so hard for most of us to tackle life's challenging situations. Why do we struggle so much when we are faced with obstacles or even just with establishing and achieving goals?

Let me ask you this: have you ever experienced that feeling of being less motivated to tackle something that required more effort, something that was uncomfortable or that you had to dig deeper for in order to achieve it? Of course you have. And, if you are like most, you may have asked yourself — why does it have to be so hard? Why can't it be easier? Why me? How can I get out of this obstacle or mess?

This is only natural and makes us all human.

There are many ways to explain this and having a background in psychology means I can draw on various schools of thought as possible hypotheses — but the simplest way of explaining it is this.

Water always takes the path of least resistance. After all, humans are over 70% water with some additional minerals and carbon. So it's not surprising that we tend to choose the path of least effort and often have to will ourselves into tackling those harder tasks.

Naturally, we tend to want to simply flow past obstacles, much like water in a little creek would more easily wash around rocks rather than over them.

However, "the rocks" in our life, those uphill stretches and challenging times are the experiences that help us to expand and grow, but this *only* takes place when we are willing to tackle them head-on, when we aren't merely wanting a free ride.

So when you are faced with an obstacle, *first* understand that it's human nature to try to avoid them. There isn't anything wrong with you, you're not flawed or weak. You are wired for the path of least resistance and are less likely to want to develop the mindset to jump over obstacles or see them as opportunities for growth. Learning to become counterintuitive to this inbuilt human conditioning is the key to success. It's what makes you superhuman.

And the good news is you can develop this new capacity to overcome obstacles instead of resist them. It's like a new muscle you can learn to strengthen.

These days, society is filled with 'instant celebrity' stories and often it's the rock stars, the movie stars and the champions that receive the most praise, admiration and envy. Many people view them as "lucky" — lucky to have fame and fortune, lucky to be talented or good-looking. Many people assume that celebrities had an easier road to success.

Yet, if we examine their journey more closely, we find that they too had to go through many trials of adversity and failure. They had to face many critics and have many setbacks. And furthermore, it was perhaps their unwavering persistent commitment to not give up that helped them reach the top of their game.

It's very easy to assume that it was simply their talent, connections or luck that made it all happen, but it's also their willingness to embrace the hard times and allow those hard times to shape them. Without doubt, this is what got them to where they are today. How many athletes do you hear suffer injury blows and have to claw their way back to the top? A lot.

So, no matter what it is that you choose, whatever you feel is your mission, pursuit or goal, remember that it is often the hard times and the challenges that edge you closer. It's all the times that you are tested to the point of almost giving up, that you are close to success.

'The breakthrough lies after the breakdown' or 'The darkest hour is just before the dawn' — these sayings are handed down through generations for a reason. Wisdom gets passed down to help the emerging generation and offer them understanding and perspective.

Consider this, if that 'testing stage' was not present then we wouldn't have any reason to dig deep and would cease to know and find our true strength and deepest commitment. We wouldn't intimately know how much we really value and believe in our dreams. But mostly, it would deprive us of our own growth. We would not grow through the process and we wouldn't feel like we fully earned the achievement. It is all for good reason if you take a wider perspective.

The skill lies in knowing this deeply and knowing how to find the strength to persist and push on when it gets tough. I even encourage people to actively look for that 'testing stage', to seek it out and smile. And the reason you can smile is because when it comes, you can know it's the indicator to show that you're on track, that you're getting closer.

But, once again, this is counterintuitive to our human nature, we want it to be easier, we want our dreams to simply flow upstream on their own accord and gently cascade around any "rocks" or challenges.

It's important to see your highest ambitions in the same light as when you make the commitment to pursue something, whether it's learning a new instrument, losing weight, building a business or achieving top marks — you do it knowing that it *will* get tough and testing. That you will have obstacles and challenges.

You cannot learn to play a piano without hitting a few wrong keys. Hitting the wrong key helps you look for the right key. If you want to get fitter, you have to challenge the plateau your body is stuck in.

Unfortunately, most people give up at these times and never find their deeper strength or feel the boost that comes from making it to the other side and achieving what they set out to do. This leaves them feeling defeated and down on themselves, little did they know how close they really were.

And, while many blame this on the comforts of our modern world or the laziness of our younger generations, it really just comes down to understanding. To know that it's human nature to seek the path of least effort. But the real signpost is the obstacle, and this itself should give us the renewed strength to go the extra distance and persist.

Ask any sporting champion and they will tell you about the dark nights of the soul, the tears and tests, about being on the cusp of giving up; they'll openly admit that it was getting through those tough times that enabled them to stand on the winner's podium.

Any successful artist will have a myriad of true tales about criticism and hardship, moments of being told they weren't good enough. Pushing on past these obstacles is what helped them earn their success and popularity.

Any entrepreneur or business owner will have had many moments of doubt and failure only to pick themselves up again and keep going to eventually succeed. Many successful businesses are only built off the back of some previous failed attempts.

And you and I, we have ample times in our own lives too. Times when we have maybe done the same. Times when we gave up too early and didn't push on to achieve something we wanted.

It is these moments that can define our lives. So, I encourage you to let your light shine and allow the light to one day shine upon you.

"I'm not afraid of storms, for I'm learning to sail my ship."
Louisa May Alcott

Trusting Ourselves to Try

Think of a newborn baby, freshly arrived and incarnated into a physical body. While we adore their innocent cuteness, they are already hard at work pushing brand-new limits and discovering an unknown world. It's not surprising that their first year is one filled with rapid intensity and growth, more than any of the following years.

At first this helpless little being requires someone to feed it, clothe it, love it and keep it warm — then gradually through trial and error it begins to sit upright, smile, communicate and play. Soon enough the little baby is feeding itself, walking and then running. This all happens from the baby trying to do things that he or she cannot yet do, and trying to do them enough times until he or she is able to do them. And then not stopping there...

Our development and will to try is only inhibited by our conditioning, the responses and comments, ideas and limitations placed upon us from the outside world. It's unnatural to stop growing and learning.

A toddler has a natural tendency to try to do

something they cannot yet do, it's only through continual 'suggestions' or 'programming' that they'll stop trying. And, we can see this as the child grows up.

Some well-meaning parents condition their child to be over-cautious, and what may begin as trying to prevent their toddler from falling over can become a way to prevent them from trying to push new boundaries. Some use negative reinforcement and unconsciously inhibit their child from trusting their true nature of striving for new advancements and abilities.

When we look at people today, too many of us are subscribed to a degree of accepted incompetence, or a fundamental belief that some people cannot move beyond their current state or level of capabilities. Perhaps, the drive, the willingness or impetus to 'try' has faded, or too much early conditioning has undermined our belief in ourselves and has eventually defeated us from attempting more challenges.

This doesn't only happen in our childhood but through all stages of life.

When we are content with something or are afraid to move beyond our current state, we stop trying. And with that, usually the drive to attempt new things, to learn, to push beyond our comfort zone and current capabilities ebbs away. There is a saying, 'If we are not green and growing, we are ripe and rotting'.

The moment that we stop striving for more, we start standing still, or in some cases, we start going backwards as everything else around us progresses forward.

With it we lose the will and the ability to tackle obstacles or problems, no matter how small or big. And, with sufficient time spent treading on the spot, attempting to expand again seems an even harder task. It can become a vicious detrimental cycle that we get stuck in.

But life is guaranteed to throw new obstacles our way, to test our will and our strength to manage them. Obstacles are here to enable us the ability to grow and flex in the face of them.

When we are doubtful and in a place of not trusting ourselves, or lack faith in our ability to rise to the occasion, too many of us will give up before trying. Yet, try we must — each and every time. After all, it is our responsibility, part of our inheritance from our ancestors, especially those who had to face much grander obstacles in order to ensure a future for us.

"Fall seven times. Stand up eight."
Japanese proverb

You Can Get Out of the Darkness — Your Ability to Respond

It can be easy to take the credit when good things happen in life, but when less desirable things happen we are often quick to blame them on circumstances, other people, bad luck, or the world. And, while I am not here to say these things are at all easy, nor should be considered as such, what I am saying is regardless of what happened and why, we are responsible for what we do with it, how we react and the attitude we foster.

It is said that life is 10% what happens to you and 90% of what you do with it. This essentially means, that we have the *response*-ability, the ability to choose, not just trigger our flight or fight response, but to mindfully choose how we want to deal with whatever life has handed us.

Sometimes of course it's much easier said than done. Just looking at some basic global statistics reveals the prevalence of people suffering within themselves.

The World Health Organization states that around 300 million people, 4.4% of the world's population are suffering from depression.[1] Globally an estimated 285 million people experienced an anxiety disorder in 2017, and around 62% of those are female.

By 2030, it is estimated that the cost to the global economy for all mental health problems could amount to $16 trillion.[2]

And furthermore, across the globe, more than 1.3 billion live in *extreme* poverty every single day. Refugees and asylum seekers, are particularly susceptible to mental health issues, it is estimated that more than 61% of refugees will experience a mental

---

1   https://www.who.int/mental_health/management/depression/en/
2   https://www.reuters.com/article/us-health-mental-global/mental-health-crisis-could-cost-the-world-16-trillion-by-2030-idUSKCN1MJ2QN
3   https://www.healthpovertyaction.org/news-events/mental-health-world-health-day-2017/

health crisis or breakdown at some stage.[3]

Then there's the innocent children, those whose lives begin with the ultimate hardship. According to UNICEF (the United Nations Children's Emergency Fund), there are at least 153 million orphans worldwide and every day, 5,700 more children become orphans. These beautiful children face huge obstacles of poverty, slavery and lack of education. They battle disease, stigma and health issues stemming from their life situation.

When it comes to these type of hard-hitting, life-changing situations, our *ability* to *respond* is very challenged. It can be the last thing you want to do.

But that's why I have written this book. Because I have discovered a formula that is guaranteed to work if you do.

I am here to tell you that a real tried-and-tested mindset and methodology can be developed regardless of what life has thrown at you.

It's the exact one I used to transform my entire life. To get out of misery and face my life alone as an orphan.

These tools, techniques and teachings lifted me out of trauma and suffering and became the foundation for creating and fulfilling my dream life.

I share them with you, not just as words to read but as a guide to help you, so you can transform your life and have the life you dreamed of.

You really can **accept, decide and dream** of the life you want. I will show you how.

Life can be different for you. It can be wonderful.

And that's why it's critical to dream of what you want because dreaming is limitless and free. It's a lifeline of hope and possibility. It shines light through the darkness.

When you have a dream, you invite something even greater — self-actualisation.

The term self-actualisation involves fulfilling your potential and being all you can be. In Chapter 8 you will see that self-actualisation is what this book is ultimately about.

"It still holds true that man is most uniquely human when he turns obstacles into opportunities."
Eric Hoffer

CHAPTER FOUR

THE WAY THROUGH ALL OBSTACLES

No one is immune to obstacles. Obstacles do not discriminate, they happen to everyone and anyone. You cannot avoid obstacles in life, even if you're from a royal family or have riches beyond measure — obstacles happen. They are a part of life.

If you think about it, since the beginning of time humans have had to face obstacles and evolve in the face of them - from natural disasters, to the threat of wild animals and disease.

Humans developed shelter, tools, weapons, hunting tactics, housing, transport, food preparations and storage, all through the ages and to our modern-day. Now we are surrounded by new technologies and conveniences.

The fact that I am sitting here today writing this book is only due to the many many generations that came before me and managed to survive the countless obstacles of their time — extreme conditions, wars, natural disasters, wild animals, ruthless leaders and diseases, to name but a few.

Over time we have continued to up the ante, we became better, smarter, more innovative at protecting and evolving ourselves. Time and time again we found better ways and new solutions for our daily challenges.

We overcame obstacles only because we helped each other and we strived to improve ourselves. It's the formula we have always used.

It's now our turn to respond. We owe it to our ancestors and our future generations to consciously strive to be better today than we were yesterday. To step up and embrace any obstacle as an opportunity for growth and evolution rather than something to complain about or worse, to let these knock us off our path or dream.

Of course, growth tends to lie outside of our comfort zone, and being comfortable can lure us into complacency or fear. Though it may seem the last thing you ever want to do — actively pushing your comfort zone in order to test yourself and edge beyond your current capabilities is a great way to expand your life, career, business, relationship and dreams.

Whether you feel it, or know it or not, our very nature is to climb from obstacle to obstacle in order to take the human race forward, day after day, year after year, generation after generation. It's what we do naturally.

So why is it then, that so many of us struggle with

even the smallest of challenges in our daily lives? How come we tend to succumb to even the minutest of pressures, crumble so quickly and give up? One just needs to look at the success rates of our New Year's resolutions to see that these days we may not display the same steadfastness to our obstacles as our ancestors did. So what happened...?

Well for one, we haven't been taught about obstacles. We haven't been educated in why obstacles are here and how best to handle them. These days, we have a lot of pressures and just getting through each day can feel like one massive obstacle in itself. A lot of people identify with their obstacles and forget that they are grander than the obstacles themselves. We are smothered in fear and low in faith.

Maya Angelou said, "I can be changed by what happens to me. But I refuse to be reduced by it."

I ask you to never let your circumstances, your life situation determine your worth or become the measurement of what you can achieve. You are far greater than you know. Do not allow circumstances to erode or reduce the power of your soul. Your dream will always overpower the obstacle if you persist.

The ADD Formula

My simple formula — the ADD formula became my pathway to success. It literally changed the course of my life and transformed my thinking. It will answer and unpack the common question of 'how'. How to turn obstacles into opportunities.

The ADD formula is designed to only ADD things to your life — good things, great things, better things. This simple formula is potent. Much like a small dose of medicine can cure big problems, so too can this small formula guarantee big success. It's called ADD because it will add to your life, not subtract. So you don't need to be afraid to follow it.

ACCEPT — Accept your failures. Accept that obstacles are everywhere. Accept that some obstacles are beyond your control. When you accept, you learn to forgive. So, accept all things now.

When you accept, you learn to forgive and you become...

Assertive – believe in yourself and your worth!

Control yourself and your emotions. Think logically and reasonably. Set clear boundaries and be decisive. Address any issues clearly and directly and don't waste time. Express your thoughts and feelings in direct and appropriate ways. Likewise, respect the thoughts, feelings, cultures and beliefs of others.

Creative – cultivate creativity by generating ideas and opinions and make something out of your great ideas and opinions. Let your imagination go wild, this allows you to think differently and uniquely. Critique yourself and set high standards. Look at things with different perspectives and use all your senses to delve and be open-minded and curious to learn and experience new ideas. Never stop formulating new ideas.

Certain – believe in yourself and your potential. Know what you like and what you want and feel it firmly in your bones.

Energetic – when you are actively working towards your purpose and dreams you are full of energy and more productive. Your energy levels go up when you're happy, inspired and feeling positive and thankful, this of course boosts your sense of achievement.

Positive – when you have a positive attitude, you always see goodness in everything and nothing is impossible. Positive people are constructive even during their tough times and always hold optimistic point of views.

Thankful (grateful) – when you are thankful and grateful you stay positive and happy. Thus, you accept obstacles or challenges openly and you free yourself from anxiety and depression. Feeling thankful can improve your health and wellbeing and your whole immune system directly or indirectly. Then you easily forgive from your heart without hesitation and that allows you to decide to move forward.

D ECIDE — Decide to move forward. Decide to pull up your socks. Decide to change. Decide to pick yourself up. You can't let obstacles beat you and cripple your future. Decide you're worth it.

When you decide it allows you to be...

Determined – Be determined to change your perspective and respond positively to failures and adversities. Determined people don't waste their time when something goes wrong, instead they focus on how they can make things better and find a better solution instead of blaming circumstances.

Explore opportunities – Explore opportunities by searching, understanding and discovering your capabilities, interests and boundaries. When you explore opportunities ensure you set a reasonable time limit so you can make decisions without lingering, and be able to assess or evaluate different opportunities that are available. Be willing to read, search and research until you are satisfied and happy with your decision.

Confident – Be confident in yourself, in your abilities and in the decisions that you are making. Trust your inner instincts and don't introduce yourself to doubts. Believe in yourself and have the courage to expose yourself to different situations, push through the uncomfortable areas so you find your limits. See things as an opportunity for challenge not a problem. Remember, the cornerstone of leadership is confidence, likewise confidence brings inspiration, success and achievement. Thus, makes you resilient to life's inevitable obstacles.

Inspired – Surround yourself with energetic and successful people. Don't waste your time and energy in little things that aren't good for you. Find inspiration from things you are passionate about and learn to be open to fresh thoughts and ideas, turning them into new-found opportunities. Create the mindset to stay receptive to inspiration by exploring new opportunities and experiences.

Diligent – Realise the value of hard work and patience. Diligent comes from the Latin term *diligere*, which means to value and take delight in, however in English it means careful and hard-working. If you are hard-working, it takes patience and you always try to do everything right and perfect. Hard work, commitment, dedication and persistent go hand-in-hand with success to achieve your dreams. This in line with the saying 'no pain, no gain'.

Embrace and love your obstacles – Find hope and meaning in every challenge or obstacles you encounter. Draw your strengths and energy through those obstacles to transform you into a better, capable, strong, resilient and successful dreamer. A successful dreamer never stops dreaming and accepts to see every obstacle as an opportunity to grow and achieve.

DREAM — Dream of a better future! Dream to succeed. Dream of your financial freedom. Dream of your vision and mission in life. Dream on! Because when you dream it gives you hope and a reason to live.

There are often many pains and so-called failures before you achieve you dreams. That's when you need to be...

Daring – Embrace struggles and be fearless. There is nothing to be afraid of, recognise fear as a hindrance to your success. Acknowledge your failures, pains and mistakes; learn from them and take action. Believe in endless possibilities and nothing is impossible with the help of God. So, conquer the fear of unknown as if it's your greatest enemy.

Resilient – When you learn to become tough either emotionally, psychologically or physically, you become resilient. Resilient people practice acceptance and patience, they don't let adversity define or break them. They look at hardship as a transition period of triumph and success. As the old metaphor says, 'resilient people are like a bamboo tree in a hurricane – they bend rather than break. They are strong and flexible with great ability to cope and find balance during difficult or stressful periods of time.'

Educate – Educate and equip yourself with the necessary knowledge and skills that you require to prepare and empower yourself to achieve your dreams. Education has the power to change lives and fuel growth and success. It helps populations and countries grow economically and flourish with prosperity.

Ambitious to achieve – It is your "can do" ambitious attitude and desire to succeed that takes you in the direction of your dreams. When you are ambitious you continuously create new dreams to achieve. You take action on your vision to change your situation to move toward better conditions. As Nelson Mandela said, "Vision without action is just a dream, action without vision just passes the time, but vision with action can change the world."

Motivated with a mission in life – It is the power to see the good within bad circumstances and adopt a positive attitude. You can't control your circumstances, but you can choose your attitude and perception towards your circumstances. That's how you can keep your motivational levels up and pursue your vision and mission during tough times. Turn obstacles into opportunities. That's how you chase your dream.

Behind every obstacle is an immense opportunity waiting for you. With this simple ADD formula, you will learn to love your obstacles and enjoy your success. And the reason I said 'love' is because in reflection the obstacle will be seen differently. You will see it as an indicator to success and the seed that grows you.

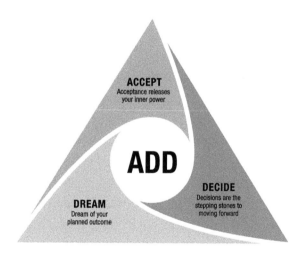

I will take you step-by-step through each area so you can relate it to your life and make the changes you need.

ACCEPT, ACCEPT, ACCEPT IT ALL

"Do not judge me by my success, judge me by how many times I fell down and got back up again."
Nelson Mandela

Society heralds success as the ultimate glory but the truth is acceptance comes before success. It was the first stepping stone to my success. Without acceptance there is no glory. That's because if we don't accept ourselves, our lives and the way things panned out for us, then we can't fully enjoy our lives and our achievements. We will still feel unconsciously unworthy and want to stay in anger, resistance or lack of forgiveness.

Acceptance was the key that unlocked the door and helped me take my first step out of misery and into a new way of life. I had to accept the very thing I didn't want to accept — that my parents were gone and it was beyond my control. That there was nothing I could do to change that harsh and devastating fact.

I had to accept the fact that my parents would no longer be there for me, to protect me, to show me affection and shower me with love, hugs, and all the basic needs that I so desperately wanted.

Though my relatives loved me like their own child, it still wasn't the same. Being with your own mother has a quality of freedom like no other. You can express what you want, when you want — a mother gets to see all sides of you. You can freely voice your likes and dislikes, your good and bad sides with no hesitation.

When you're with someone else, you are trying to be a good girl or boy, a good person because you don't want to upset them. Even if you want to say no, you often don't directly come out and say it because you want to be polite and respectful. So that's the difference. And all these little and big things, I had to accept fully. I had to accept the fact my life would never be the same, that I wouldn't be the same person I once was. I was an orphan and because of that my life wouldn't return back to normal. I had to accept that some things change forever.

Some of my siblings didn't arrive at that level of acceptance and that's the reason some of them didn't move forward. They couldn't accept their situation. But you can't cry over spilled milk. It's done. You only set yourself up to suffer if you don't accept what has already happened.

What is done is done and the only thing left is to live and accept it.

Some things are out of your control and no matter how you feel, or what you think about it, it won't change the ultimate fact. Being from a minority group is something I accept, for if we don't accept our own lives and ourselves then how can we expect anyone else to accept us?

There are many great motivational speakers who have had very challenging life situations. Some are in wheelchairs, some have disfigured bodies or faces, some have mental issues that are life-long. The reason they have become inspirational is because they accepted their situation, it doesn't mean they love it or wish it hadn't happened but they accepted their fate and decided to do something positive about it.

I'll say it again, unless you accept your life condition, you cannot make a decision to change.

Acceptance is very, very important. Once you have accepted your situation you can fully make a decision about which direction to take, or you can also choose to stay right where you are now. Whichever decision you make, be happy and accept it, otherwise it will haunt you and you'll never move forward.

To live a new life, you must accept that your 'old life' or 'that event' which occurred, happened. And yes, maybe it was horrible and devastating – but it happened and no amount of suffering will change that. And though certainly things won't be the same as before, at least you can come to terms with accepting it. Then give yourself permission to be happy, regardless of whether you decide to move forward or stay where you are, but at least be happy with your decision.

Whatever decision you make is *your* choice. If you decide to stay in misery then at least be happy with your miserable choice.

But if you choose to be happy *and* move forward, then go for it and keep moving, because life is very short and you have got to enjoy it. You have only one life so live that life to the maximum. Be limitless.

Acceptance allows you to move freely in the world

and live more fearlessly. It's the step that needs to happen *before* action and decision-making because it gives you the ultimate clarity in order to make better decisions.

Acceptance also breeds forgiveness. Forgiveness is an active ingredient that changes you. As Bernard Meltzer pointed out, "When you forgive, you in no way change the past — but you sure do change the future."

Accept your circumstances, accept the conditions you currently face. Then forgive. Forgive whoever you need to, forgive life, forgive yourself. And yes, it's often hard. It's a true act of strength and courage. That's why Gandhi said, "The weak can never forgive. Forgiveness is the attribute of the strong."

He's right, forgiveness is for the strong, but you are strong and you can forgive.

> *"Forgiveness is not always easy. At times it feels more painful than the wound we suffered, to forgive the one that inflicted it. And yet, there is no peace without forgiveness."*
> **Marianne Williamson**

Whatever happened, it's a part and parcel of life. There are a lot of emotions involved. Sometimes we are happy, sometimes we are sad and depressed. Some people have anxiety, others are paralysed by fear. Regardless of the limiting emotion, the first technique is to accept that it's present and it's holding you back. Accept that you may need help to move forward. Accept that you are free to make new and different choices if you need to.

It's also important to accept the fact that wonderful things can happen too. That dreams can come true. That you can be happy. That you can change for the better.

It can be really hard to accept things that make no sense. Or accept judgement from others. You don't need to accept what other people think or say about you. You only need to accept that they have the freedom to think and say whatever they want. You may have to accept that they are negative toxic people trying to bring you down. Acceptance helps release judgement, hate and anger and makes room for healing and forgiveness, both yourself and other people. Acceptance is a practical tool to free yourself from stress.

One of the hardest things to do is to accept a condition or circumstance when it's complex and strong emotions are involved. However, acceptance isn't to surrender and agree wholeheartedly with your situation, it's to see it objectively for what it is, enabling you to make smart and often necessary decisions to move forward. It allows you to be more rational than emotional and let go of what you cannot control. When your emotion supersedes your logic or reasoning, you need to step back and remind yourself to recognise that we are all human beings and are created with our cognition higher than our emotion.

If you think about it, our brain is positioned at the highest section of our body, and our heart is below our brain. Therefore, we should not allow fleeting emotions to dictate our logical thinking. We must make informed and critical decisions in chasing our dreams.

It wasn't easy for me when I first came to Australia. It was a new country and I was unmistakably foreign to many. I experienced judgement from some people due to the fact that I was from a different place, a cultural minority and that I am a Muslim woman who wears a headscarf. Some thought I was a nun, whereas others thought I was a terrorist. These two extreme and completely opposing judgements could happen in the one day.

However, people's views and judgements did not break me, they did not reduce my capabilities or my determination to make a contribution to society. Instead, they strengthened and defined me beyond my wildest dreams.

Like anyone, I cannot control how other people see me, or what they believe about me. Their thoughts and ideas are their prerogative, they are free to think and feel how they wish. But I have control of my attitude, my behaviour, my perception and my decisions. And that's why I also love to dream because no one can take that from you.

Even from an early age, I could see that my ethnic, cultural, minority background, meant that I needed to assimilate with a diverse group of friends to become part of the whole. Being a minority was an obstacle I had to face growing up. I remember once when I was young, we went on a holiday in Cebu (one of the cities in the Philippines). I was often asked where I was from. I would explain that I was from Marawi City, a city in Mindanao where the majority of people are Muslims. Most people wanted to know if I was a Muslim too, or a Muslim nun.

My headscarf alone would discriminate my identity according to what each person believed. My headscarf couldn't go unnoticed and it became the target of many questions and judgements.

I would quote Kemi Sogunle to myself, "The tests we face in life's journey are not to reveal our weaknesses but to help us discover our inner strengths. We can only know how strong we are when we strive and thrive beyond the challenges we face."

Furthermore, being a woman and of an ethnic cultural background made it difficult for job opportunities. When I came to Australia in 1998 and settled down after marriage, I remember being so desperate for a job to make ends meet that I did everything to become employed. My husband was working and our first son was born in 1999, we couldn't afford to buy our son a new shirt or a toy. I borrowed toys from the library in order to keep my son busy, and I would go to different companies and organisations handing in my resume hoping for any position that would merit my qualification.

I got frustrated many times as no one would even look at my resume. In a way, I was not disappointed because I wasn't expecting a company to offer me a job. I knew and understood how tough the situation was. However, this made me even stronger and helped me to keep going and not give up.

As Rikki Rogers said "Strength doesn't come from what you can do. It comes from overcoming the things you once thought you couldn't." I held strong to my inner vision.

To broaden my employment opportunities, I started another Master's degree in Education and Training at Victoria University in the evening when my husband returned home from work.

On a dark winter's night on 9 July 2003 around 6:00 pm as I was walking towards the university to attend my night time classes. I could hear male voices calling "Hey...you terrorist!" At first, I was confused to where these voices were coming from and to whom it was directed. I looked around for the voices. I felt scared and vulnerable walking alone at night. My heart began to race.

Looking around, I could barely see anyone but the voices were growing louder and closer repeating the words "Hey, you terrorist!" I suddenly saw three massive men opposite me as I was about to cross the road. I shut my eyes and my body started to shake. My knees were trembling and I could barely support my body.

I collected my strength and energy and prepared to run but an inner strength suddenly came from within me. My body and mind switched into survival mode, I gathered my strength within and I said to them with firm strong voice, "What made you call me a terrorist? Did I kill any of your family members for you to label me a terrorist?"

I could not comprehend where my strength and courage came from. Receiving no response from them, I briskly walked, almost ran, to get out of that situation as quickly as possible. I set toward the safety zone of the University campus.

When I reached my classroom, I was absolutely terrified. My whole body was shaking and could barely catch my breath. I was very disturbed during my class and could not pay attention to my lecturer's class discussion. Before the end of the lecture I had to leave the classroom to make a phone call to my husband to fetch me from my classroom at 9:30 pm immediately after my class. I was also pregnant with my third child and he had to drag our two sleepy toddler children out of the house with him at night.

This experience disturbed me for a few weeks, and all because I was perceived differently with a headscarf.

I had to accept that some obstacles were beyond my control. I couldn't control what people thought of Muslim women wearing headscarves or the way other people treated me.

From then onwards, I was terrified to take public transport or walk alone. But my dream was bigger than my fear and we found ways to cope.

My husband, along with our two toddler children, dropped me right at the door of my university classroom every time I attended. Together they waited three hours in the car park in order to pick me up when my class finished. Graduating from university really was a team effort. Without the support of my husband and children, graduating would have been an exceptionally difficult task.

In 2002, for a long period of time, I could not get a job nor a childcare place for my son. I felt like I had hit yet another big obstacle. Yet we were also getting used to turning obstacles into opportunities.

My husband and I decided to establish our own childcare and kindergarten centre. It was a great challenge I can assure you. I had never run a business in my life and I was in a new country without any experience in business. On top of that, I was an unemployed migrant, Muslim woman trying to establish a new business.

We pro-actively turned another obstacle into a massive opportunity, not just for ourselves but for the community. My son had quality child care, and I became the Managing Director of our business. This allowed us to provide job opportunities for those who could not get jobs, people like me.

With this achievement, I was also able to create more job opportunities and established educational institutions in Australia and the Philippines. I even won the Australia 2018 AusMumpreneur Multicultural Business Excellence Award.

All this through using my simple ADD formula.

You would think that being a woman from a minority

ethnic background would be more than enough for one to handle. That's three demerit points of being 'disadvantaged'. But these three 'obstacles' didn't break me, they defined, strengthened and cemented me firmly into my own sense of self. They helped make me who I am today. And your obstacles and differences make you unique and can define you too.

George Bernard Shaw said, "People are always blaming their circumstances for what they are. I don't believe in circumstances. The people who get on in this world are the people who get up and look for the circumstances they want, and if they can't find them, make them."

I agree. Accept and be confident and proud of who you are. You're unique. Take every challenge or obstacle along the way and take courage in the words of Margaret Thatcher who said, "You may have to fight a battle more than once to win it."

During a recent event, I was fortunate to have a wonderful conversation with a truly inspirational woman, Dr. Tererai Trent, the author of *The Awakened Woman — Remembering & Reigniting Our Sacred Dreams* and the woman Oprah called her "all-time favourite guest." We were at Crown in Melbourne (2018) and Tererai said that women are like bamboo trees, both strong and flexible. That when a strong wind blows, the bamboo swings and sways left and right, forward and backward but then they always go back gracefully to their original position when the wind stops. She said that women never break like bamboo trees.

I survived those colourful obstacles in my life only because they forced me to stand on the ground like a flexible bamboo tree, swinging and swaying in the wind and yet returning to my original self after every storm.

I see women do this every day and yet they are unaware of their incredible flexibility and beauty.

Acceptance is an attitude. A way of life that can embrace you like a warm hug.

Accept yourself in all your glory, your circumstances, your past and all the decisions you made along the way.

Accepting will free you for the next step....and that is to DECIDE.

⟵ I ACCEPT ⟶

Write down things you can accept (and must accept) to move forward in your life.

....
....
....
....
....
....
....
....
....
....
....
....
....
....
....
....
....
....
....

"Time does not heal everything but acceptance will heal everything."

CHAPTER FIVE

THE POWER TO DECIDE

Without direction, we go nowhere. It is said that if you don't know where you are going any road will lead you there.

This raises the importance of having direction, a goal, aim or mission that makes you head toward a defined goal or outcome. Mind you, you don't necessarily need to know 'how' to get there, but 'why' you want to get there. Then everything else will emerge and the stepping stones you need in order to get there will appear.

You may not be able to make all decisions yet, but there is one major decision that you can make. And that is to decide to move forward. To not stay stuck and complaining. Decisions equal personal power.

DECIDE

We can't let obstacles hold us back and cripple us for

the rest of our life. We need to let go of what's holding us back. Sometimes we may decide on something that we deem as a small and inconsequential decision but it could in fact be life-altering. Decisions are powerful, even the seemingly 'small' ones can have huge ripple effects.

In 1991, I was accepted to International Islamic University (IIU) in Malaysia on a scholarship for my Bachelor Degree. It was very difficult for me to make the decision and my uncle and aunty's family had reservations about me leaving. What was holding me back was the feeling of uncertainty. My uncle and aunty were worried about my safety and well-being and considered not letting me go because they were responsible for my wellbeing and they did not want to take the blame from other relatives if something were to happen to me. I almost missed the opportunity. Thankfully, I assessed the scholarship opportunity again and I knew I had to decide. I tried to convince them to let me go the night before a flight to Malaysia was available. I didn't have a ticket and it was such a small window of time, but deep down I couldn't let uncertainty stop me from trying to better my future. The decision for me to go was made at midnight. I had to leave the house at 5:00 am so I could purchase my ticket prior to my departure. I did not realise at the time that going to Malaysia would change the course of my life and open doors to many opportunities. But all decisions are stepping-stones. Some are monumental leaps and others may be one small step, yet if they propel you forward then they're worth it. Remember decisions are your personal tool of power.

"Nothing happens until you decide. Make a decision and watch your life move."
Oprah Winfrey

We previously talked about how we are largely water, and that water will travel along the easiest pathway unless you funnel it in a particular way. If you don't give it a pathway, it will simply spill out in any and all directions. This is similarly true for our thoughts, our energy, our time, our careers and how we focus. Unless we define where we want to go. And, by that I mean define it *exactly*, with clarity and certainty, then just like water, if you channel your energy with intention — it will flow in that direction.

You can guide water to flow evenly toward your goal, or you can narrow the flow like a funnel and the more defined you make it, the stronger the flow gets. If you push water through a narrow passage or pipe, it turns into a jet stream. Now, if you do the same with your goals, and aims and refine them, you can sharpen your energy like a laser. If you spend the most productive time of the day with your focused energy and clearly defined goals and vision, you can create powerful outcomes – just like a jet stream or laser beam.

The problem is that many of us are like a boat without a rudder, swayed by the wind and the waves, endlessly drifting and bopping in the currents of life, tossed around by the wind that changes direction all the time. To decide is not easy and it can be frightening, especially when you're not entirely certain nor have clarity of your vision and direction. Without a clearly defined vision or mission, or without a purpose, we can be more easily influenced by anything that comes our way. See, much like water will flow the path of least resistance, our nature is to flow with the currents and that may not take us closer to where we want to go. Unless we are forced to go through the challenges and struggles of pushing uphill, squeezing through tight passages and being bashed up against the banks, our pathways will simply take the easy way.

Finding your mission, committing to your aim or goal, essentially puts a rudder on your boat. It gives you direction, the ability to steer in a direction. The more defined we can make our goal, the more likely we have a keel, a rudder and even a sail to get us there in a more direct and faster fashion.

It does not however mean that we won't encounter strong opposing winds, waves and currents. But steering in your direction means you will actually ride these waves toward where you are going.

This means that finding your very own vision and mission, your purpose in life is paramount to setting sail in that direction. Without defining what it is you want and why, you will simply go in any direction or be easily swayed off your course.

Let us say you want to make a difference in the world for young women. There are multiple ways of doing so. But, if you want to reach and affect the lives of many young women in the world, you need to find a way to expand your reach. Unless you define what that looks like, and the outcomes this brings, the impact it shall have and the change it can bring to future generations, you will not find your path easily. In fact, you'll see many general roads will lead you there or lead you off your path.

When you clearly define the way you want to have impact, let's say speaking to young women, you have to think clearly about how you do that. You need to assess the age group, the location, the cultural groups, the socio-economic disposition, their goals and needs. As you define things more clearly, the pathway becomes clearer and you will meet people and come across opportunities and ways to get you there faster. You just need to know the *where* and *why* — and the *how* will come.

It's easy to get stuck when you focus on the *how*, as often this doesn't come immediately but when you have clarity of what you want and accept whatever consequences that may come along with it, the *how* begins to unfold.

You might start helping in a refuge, or speak with teens at schools and universities, or perhaps attend specific conferences and groups. Then you may start connecting with like-minded people and recognise the sort of qualifications that can elevate you to your goal. You might start speaking at small events and to groups here and there, collate some key issues, ideas and solutions and soon produce a flyer or memo. Perhaps, you even get commentary from key influencers in this area and later publish a book.

Now, that you're a published author and speaker on the topic, you might visit schools and universities, collaborate with communities and women's projects and engage a public relations or media agency to get your message out further and build your profile.

Before long, you are seen and are recognised as an important voice in the field and people want to hear you speak or get comments from you, and you are becoming a go-to expert.

Your book reaches beyond the confines of the core interest groups and you can raise awareness and all of a sudden you are on TV and radio, in newspapers and get invited to present to large audiences. All this cannot happen, unless you define clearly what it is you really want to do.

So, what is your mission, vision and your purpose?

What is your why?

Why do you feel drawn to this?

If you want to donate or build orphanages, a school, feed people, provide safe spaces for women or access to health services or education. Just, define what it is that *really* drives you, and then go for that.

If it is money that motivates you, where do you want

to use the money and what it is for?

Put that rudder on, set your sail and know that you will encounter opposing winds, tides and waves, expect that at some stage you will feel like turning back, you'll feel sick to your stomach and consider giving up. Expect it so it doesn't surprise you.

You need to be ready for those hindrances and obstacles. Know deep in your inner being that there is no way you will give up. And, then you will discover the strength, the power and the will to go through whatever it takes. There will be lot of pain-points and failures to go through but you need to anticipate and expect them so you can be well prepared to face them.

You then know that the path you travel in pursuit of your highest mission is not going to be easy or straight like a stylised growth chart. You will happily travel the ups and downs, the back and forth, squiggles and turn-abouts along the way that will ultimately lead you closer to your dream.

The harder it gets, the closer you know you are getting. And, despite the obstacles and tests, you know deep down there is no wavering and it is here that you meet that depth of your inner strength — your resilience.

Unless you test yourself to this extent, you will not peel back the layers to find it. But, once you do, you can transmute the toughest of situations and obstacles that may and will come your way.

Of course, if you are not committed and don't have a deeply rooted mission, vision or purpose, any obstacles will sway you off your target. Unless you are willing and knowingly prepared to do and embrace whatever it takes, you are likely to slip away from your aim, much like many people do these days.

There is no judgement in this, we are, after all just human. Yet, in that humanness also lies the capacity to work hard and find the resilience within.

There are hundreds and thousands, even millions of people — women, men and children that have dug deep and found the strength that was needed to push beyond and make a difference — be it in their own life, that of those closest to them or further afield in the community, city, country or the world.

Decisions Shared Can Halve the Burden

Nine years ago, approximately a year after my fourth child was born, I woke up in the morning feeling very sick. My heart was palpitating and my whole body was shaking and aching. I felt anxious, short of breath and a huge pain tightened in my chest. My husband, Hassan, had to call an ambulance and I was taken to the hospital.

On the way to the hospital the ambulance had to pull over on the side of the road to stabilise my health condition as I was drifting. In the hospital, the doctors conducted several blood tests to better understand my health condition. I was released on the same day from the hospital without a diagnosis.

From that moment, my health started to deteriorate day by day. I was seeing my doctor almost every second day and she was referring me to different specialists.

My doctor suspected a few possibilities — vitamin B4, B6 and B12 deficiency; goiter; cancer; heart problems, etc. She didn't give up on me. She sent me from specialist to specialist both locally and abroad. My medical tests were as thick as a book and all of them came back negative. I had consulted heart doctors, gynaecologists, ophthalmologists, ENT doctors, endocrinologists and many more.

None of those doctors could diagnose my medical condition and most of them were referring me to see a psychologist or prescribing anti-depressant medicine. I would normally argue that my psychologist background gave me sound reasoning to refute their claims that I needed to see psychologist or to take anti-depressant medication. Some believed that I was burnt out from work and over-stressed.

One day I fainted while in the clinic. My doctor had to call an ambulance to take me to the hospital. In the hospital different blood tests were conducted to further investigate my health status and test for different cancers.

At the end of the day, I was once again released from the hospital without a diagnosis. All results indicated that I had no medical problems. Though I was physically unwell and could barely feed myself, I couldn't even lift up a glass to drink water.

I had neglected my duty of care and responsibilities towards my family. Especially to my one-year-old daughter, Dania. I could not even prepare her food and milk. Nor could I bath and change her.

On one occasion, she was playing around me while I was sitting on our couch at home. She wanted a hug from me and demanded that I lift her up from the ground and carry her around, as toddlers would normally do. But I just couldn't. She threw herself on the floor crying. I tried to lift her again but I just couldn't do it, I cried with her. My health was deteriorating and getting worse every day, I looked miserable and felt devastated!

The following day I had an appointment with an endocrinologist (a doctor specialised in goiter problems), he checked my throat and other parts of my body and at the end of the session he hammered the heels and soles of my feet.

He looked at me, the ghost-like figure in front of him and said, "Mrs. Younes, I could not see any sign of a goitre or any medical abnormalities. Everything is normal."

He then asked me, "How old is your youngest child?" I told him she is more than a year. He looked at me and shook his head softly, "You may have Post Natal Syndrome Disorder."

He went on to tell me that there's no medicine for it! I looked at him blankly. I had never heard of this disorder.

"How long will it take for me to recover?" I asked.

"I don't know, maybe 2 weeks, 6 months, 15 years or more. I can't tell you! You just have to accept that you need to live with it and there is no medication."

I looked at my husband with tears rolling down my face. Hassan reached for my hand and said, "Let's go home".

We got in the car, both of us silent for almost an hour whilst driving back home.

Halfway home, I told Hassan, "Hon, we have to accept the reality. I don't think I can make it any longer. I've been sick for more than three months and my health is deteriorating each day. We need to prepare for the worse. I may make it and I may not. If something happens to me, I have two requests from you. First, I want you to remarry — I don't want you to feel lonely, you need someone to look after you and love you. Secondly, please don't neglect our children especially little Dania. Look after them no matter what happens. If you struggle with Dania, let my niece, Raisa, look after her."

Hassan looked at me and said, "Hon, you're not going anywhere and you are not leaving us yet. We will be raising our children together the way we want them to be raised. And I want you to be strong. I'm here for you. It doesn't matter what it takes."

Hassan continued, "And you know Hon, I've already made my decision that if something happened to you, I will never remarry. I promise you that I will look after our kids no matter what".

My husband had to quit his job to look after me throughout my sickness and recovery period. It was a huge sacrifice but he was beside me 24 hours a day lifting up my morale, boosting my confidence and self-esteem. Despite the fact that some days I was like a lifeless body, just weak laying there. He would look after me and on the days that I couldn't move, he would take me outside to get some sun and fresh-air. His care was my medicine.

Though our business was struggling to make ends meet, he chose to be beside me, to support me and give me the strength and courage that I needed to recover. It was his presence, his undivided attention and unconditional love that sped up my recovery and helped me heal.

We went through countless obstacles, long periods of frustration, disappointment, emotional and financial hardships, but we made it through. My recovery took around one year, but recovery happened. I did finally get better.

We learnt to love each other more deeply. To turn those obstacles into opportunities and use them to our advantage. Those obstacles made our marriage and our whole family dynamic stronger and solid. They defined and strengthened us and our children.

Hassan and I accepted the obstacle of my ill-health, that there was no medicine for my illness, but we decided to move forward, to support each other and not let my illness hold us back. We wanted the recovery to happen so we could function normally, raise our children together and make a difference to their future. Deciding together halved the pressure and gave me the wings to fly forward.

I decided to move forward and free myself from

ill-health and the toll it took regardless of how long it would take. I couldn't let those obstacles hold me back and cripple my future. I decided to use this hard experience to grow stronger, more independent and resilient. Many times I thought that I was failing but facing toward the obstacles and not away from them made all the difference.

"Two roads diverged in a wood and I - I took the one less traveled by, and that has made all the difference."
Robert Frost

The School of Life
School and education are important, but, life has this ability to teach us through experience. We are all attending the School of Life. And it's here in the School of Life that obstacles arrive no matter who you are or what background you have. My experience with postnatal syndrome wasn't due to a lack of education, it was due to life.

School is like the theoretical part of your driver's license. Unless you get in the car and actually start driving and apply your theory in practical ways you will not actually get to know what it is like to drive. Nor will you get anywhere. What I am trying to say is that by living we get to add to our understanding, we have experiences to draw on and we get to learn how to rely on our innate abilities in deeper ways.

This is when real learning takes place and where resilience is developed.

Throughout my education, I was perhaps fortunate enough to have teachers that inspired and motivated me to do my best and to try for scholarships which would eventually open doors. But it all stemmed from the point of *deciding*. *Deciding* that I was the only one able to make any difference in my life. If I wanted something better, I was the one, the only one who could make this happen. Support, good teachers and encouragement were all additional bonuses.

"Don't entrust your future on others' hands. Rather make decisions by yourself with the help of God's guidance. Hold your beliefs so tight and never let go of them!"
Hark Herald Sarmiento

+++

"When someone makes a decision, he is really diving into a strong current that will carry him to places he had never dreamed of when he first made the decision."
Paulo Coelho

+++

Decisions lead to personal growth

When you make a decision to move forward — you will grow. Growth always happens outside of our comfort zone and if you reflect back on the times when you really expanded, or achieved things beyond what you thought you were capable of, they occurred when you were challenged. Yes, outside your comfort zone. But why is this and what really goes on?

We've all heard about the fight or flight response in our reptilian brain. Well, much like that, the moment we feel safe, comfortable and relaxed, we operate on a different energy than if we are stressed or challenged.

They say, 'necessity is the mother of invention' and nothing could be truer. If life throws us situations that demand more of us, we first flick into the alert and tense mode. You know the one that lets us climb mountains or lift amazing weights, work endless hours to meet a deadline and so on.

But it does not stop there. If we are really faced with obstacles in our life that at first seem impossible to manage or overcome, we can just as easily get overwhelmed and crumble under the challenge of it, be it perceived or real.

For many, when we are faced with major obstacles, we will give up in the face of the situation. And, of course if we think something is too big or too insurmountable to overcome, then it most certainly will be. However, there are more and more people like Nelson Mandela, Oprah Winfrey, Mother Teresa and Martin Luther King, Jr., that rise to the occasion, who treat obstacles as an opportunity to exercise resilience. For these folks, when problems arise they thrive. They look at those obstacles as stepping stones to success and toward achieving their dreams.

But, of course we are not all the same, some of us manage problems better than others. The underlying premise is this, if we are committed to be our best and to become better tomorrow than we were yesterday, then our today is already pre-set to embrace obstacles and change as a way to grow. And, we would also innately know that this growth cannot be without discomfort or pain.

Take the gym for an example. You might want to lose a few kilograms or gain some muscle. If you go and work out only occasionally and you stay well within your comfort zone, either nothing will happen or it will happen very slowly. Yet, when you push yourself, go hard and take your workout further out of your comfort zone — you will see results. You know you will sweat, you will be sore, and it will hurt to do those extra lifts, lunges or push-ups, the ones beyond the number you know you can do, but you will see a difference.

If you talk to high-performance athletes, entrepreneurs and those committed to lifelong learning and personal growth, they will tell you that the darkest hour is just before the dawn. That the breakthrough is just after the breakdown. If you can push yourself beyond despair, beyond the point of wanting to give up you get to the other side of pain.

When you ask yourself *why? what for? why me?* — when you think that it's all too hard and you're losing your will, strength or capacity — that's the best indicator that you're about to have a breakthrough. That is when you grow the most and often leap forward. That's when new opportunities and possibilities open up before you. Just like they did for me.

Decisions are powerful things. They are meant to change you. They aren't always easy...in fact they're supposed to alter life, that's why you made them in the first place. You made them to change your life.

So, decisions should not be delayed too long, otherwise you will let doubt and worry kill your decision over time. There are times when you make decisions quickly and leave no room for confusion, doubt and worry.

> *"Some of our important choices have a time line.*
> *If we delay a decision, the opportunity is gone forever.*
> *Sometimes our doubts keep us from making a choice that*
> *involves change. Thus, an opportunity may be missed."*
> **James E. Faust**

"It is very important to know who you are. To make decisions. To show who you are."
Malala Yousafzai

⤙ DECISIONS I CAN MAKE ⤚
TO MOVE FORWARD
IN MY LIFE

"
May your choices
reflect your hopes,
not your fears. "
Nelson Mandela

Sarifa High School graduation from Mindanao State University – Science High School (MSU-SHS) Marawi City, Philippines

Sarifa's Elementary graduation fro MSU-ILS, Marawi City Philippines

Sarifa and Cora High school photo

Sarifa graduating from International Islamic University in Malaysia (IIUM)

Sarifa during high school graduation receiving her high school certificate

Sarifa and Cora one of the weekends during high school

Hassan and Sarifa in Malaysia

Sarifa and Hassan's Wedding (1998)

Sarifa and Hassan's Wedding (1998)

L-R: Ali Younes (Hassan's father); Hassan; Sarifa; Sarah and
Dumarpa Macarambon (Sarifa's adopted parents) wedding photo

Sarifa and Hassan during Sarifa's graduation
(Master's Degree in Education and Training) at
Victoria University, Australia

Sarifa, Hassan and Adam (eldest son)

Sarifa's children : Nahda, Adam and Ahmad in Tasmania

Sarifa during Australia citizenship ceremony in 2005

Sarifa at the 2018 AusMumpreneur Multicultural Cultural Business Excellence Awards

Sarifa, Hassan and their four children

Sarifa at the 2018 AusMumpreneur Multicultural Cultural Business Excellence Awards

Sarifa and Hassan at the 2018 AusMumpreneur Multicultural Cultural Business Excellence Awards

4th Wedding Anniversary

7th Wedding Anniversary

Sarifa with Dr. Terarai Trent

Sarifa with Dr. Terarai Trent

Sarifa with Dean Publishing,
Susan Dean and Natalie Deane

The family (L-R): Adam (eldest child); Sarifa; Nahda (2nd child);
Dania (4th child/youngest); Ahmad (3rd child); and Hassan

CHAPTER SIX

DREAMING IS FREE

It's beautiful to dream. When you dream, you have a purpose in life and dreams give you hope and reasons to live. Dreams create huge waves of positive energy inside of us.

When people don't have a dream, they become expired. To expire is to take breath out from life. When people expire, they don't see meaning in life. The breath is taken out of life. There's no vitality and passion. When products are expired they are considered past their effective date.

DREAM

Harriet Tubman said, "Every great dream begins with a dreamer. Always remember, you have within you the strength, the patience, and the passion to reach for the stars to change the world."

You are the dreamer of your life and you can dream whatever your heart desires.

When I became an orphan, I had to start thinking about the type of future I would have without a proper education. It wasn't promising.

Growing up in a country that could not provide enough employment opportunities for its population worried me, particularly for those who are disadvantaged by their circumstances, those like me.

With a heavy population of over 95 million people, decent job opportunities are rare. I had to start thinking from a young age about how could I rise above these challenges knowing that I had no parents to support or finance my dreams. I also didn't have to look too far to see the living conditions of the growing population, it was alarming to say the least and fuelled my desire for a better life.

The only hope for me was education. It was my only way out. If I wanted to live a decent life, I needed an education. It is a survival of the fittest. As Nelson Mandela said, "Education is the most powerful weapon which you can use to change the world."

I also later discovered that many men and women who graduated from universities didn't necessarily get jobs. Many were very lucky if they were able to seek job opportunities in other countries like Saudi Arabia, United Arab Emirates, United Kingdom, United States etc.

Getting an opportunity to study in Malaysia was a rare opportunity and one I knew I had to seize and grab with both hands. Going to Malaysia opened up many new opportunities for me. It was exciting and yet challenging. I had countless challenging experiences from food, friends, lecturers, cultures, and learning the academic differences between the American and British systems.

Despite all these challenges and obstacles along the way, I knew that I needed to be tough, inspired, and optimistic. I had a dream and a purpose in life. As success coach Rob Laino said, "If you expect life to be easy, challenges will seem difficult. If you accept that challenges may occur, life will be easier."

Deep down the only thing that really pushed me to dream was because I didn't want a life that was limiting. I didn't want to have that type of life. I didn't want my fate sealed due to lack of education and opportunity. But this would be the case if I just flowed with the stream of life and didn't try swim upstream.

For me, life without education limited me, not just as an individual but as a woman and an active member of society. It would mean that I wouldn't be able to intelligently discuss many topics with my family, community or society. My dream of getting an education to pull myself out of misery also meant that I could contribute intellectually around the community, I could impact other people's lives also. I could be armed with more knowledge and better decision-making skills.

My dream continues today. It's to help, to be of service, and because I went through life needing help, I could both sympathise and empathise with those people who are disadvantaged by their circumstances. Thus, I vowed that one day I would help others too. My dream is to educate, inspire, empower and help orphans, women, young people and anyone disadvantaged by their circumstances to realise their dreams.

Naturally, the best way I believe to help disadvantaged populations to realise their dreams and turn their obstacles into opportunities is through education. An educated population means equipping disadvantaged men, women, children and orphans with avenues and possibilities to sharpen their talents and skills. This allows them to participate and contribute to the country's productivity and economic growth. A well-educated population means a peaceful society, a society that breeds dreamers, both big and small.

We can have both small dreams and big dreams. They are equally valuable and work together.

Small dreams are your immediate needs and they are pathways to your big dreams. Your dreams motivate you and push you to pursue your interest and discover your potentials. When you keep dreaming, you keep receiving too.

Big dreams are those which require planning and strategies to achieve long-term success in the future.

It is free to dream that's why I continue to dream big dreams. It doesn't cost a single cent yet it supplies you with so much. Being an orphan, I had nothing but a dream.

I encourage people of all ages to dream. Dreaming isn't for children, it's for everyone.

Dr. Tererai Trent calls big dreams "The Great Hunger". She said that "without a burning desire to change the trajectory of my life and move toward a purposeful life, I would still be leading an unfulfilled life in my village."

In an inspiring speech given at Oklahoma State University, Dr. Tererai Trent spoke about the power of dreams and education. She told the graduates about the two types of hunger. She said, "There is small hunger that wants immediate gratification. There is great hunger for a meaningful life, social justice and peace. Go into the world and make a difference. Let that great hunger drive you."

It was this great hunger that stirred within me. Tapped at my soul and begged to be released.

In 2008, Hassan and I welcomed our fourth child. That's when my passion for education grew even stronger. The great hunger I had for education stemmed from my belief that a well-educated population means a productive and peaceful society.

It was this passion and obsession that prompted my husband and I to dream big. Very big.

In 2013, we established our first school in the Philippines, The International Academy of Marawi. This school provides education from kindergarten to Year 12.

We ensure that our students and our local community are given the opportunities in education, knowledge and skills at an international level. The vision for International Academy of Marawi is to be "A School of Distinction" in the Philippines and to be internationally recognised for its high standards and quality education. The school is intended to always be a special place of learning and we endeavour to implement the best quality practices.

International Academy of Marawi was accredited with the department of Education in the Philippines. We are currently working on becoming the benchmark for an independent school in Mindanao to have the choice of the highest standard required for the International Baccalaureate Programme.

School to us is not just about education, it's a place to belong and grow. It's a haven for development in all areas — social, intellectual, and emotional.

The school helps our students access a broad range of knowledge, skills and competencies, and also promotes a set of values and attitudes that will enable them to become more resilient and ready for the dynamic world, whether local or abroad. We encourage a sense of community development and promote a sense of global citizenship.

We believe that this student-centered approach is the best way for students to:
- Achieve their academic potential
- Be caring, reflective learners
- Become global-minded citizens
- Lead healthy and balanced lives

We also believe that the best way to stay centered in life is with good values.

Our school values are consistent with the school

motto: "God, advance me in Knowledge".

These values and attributes consist of:

- Respect
- Responsibility
- Honesty and integrity
- Cooperation, and
- Perseverance

The school established an International Students Program in 2015 and has long-standing relationships with schools and Training Colleges in Australia.

We are so proud to have a culturally diverse student body where students work and socialise together in harmony and with mutual respect. This is a deeper education in itself.

Two years after we established our first school, in 2015, my husband and I established a training organisation in Melbourne that offers Certificate III and Diploma in Early Childhood Education and other courses.

I realised that some of the educators we employed were not completely competent to deliver high-quality programs and education for our children. So, I decided to re-train and equip them and other students with the necessary skills and knowledge they required for their job.

Nurturing dreams comes in many different ways and I believe it's all our duty to care, encourage and develop our citizens. If someone needs more skills and we can provide them with that, then it's a win-win-win situation. They win, you win, the world wins.

Take some women as an example, many did not get the childhood chance to be educated, but we cannot say that it's too late or too bad now. We can do something, we can empower them now to gain some new skills and tools. It may not come through formal education as that's not always a viable option for some, but we can at least give them new skills and tools so they can have a proper life. When you don't have a proper life, it's like you're dead, you're hardly breathing and life can become very tough and meaningless.

Positive Energy Keeps the Dreams Burning

I always tell our staff at the childcare centres and schools that to have continuous positive energy, you have to keep nurturing that energy. You have to keep feeding that buzzing energy with your dreams and the positive people around you.

To nurture and keep our dreams alive and buzzing, to help them grow and thrive is only achieved by pouring a lot of love into them. This means feeding your dream with positive energy and thought aspirations and passion. Never pollute your positive thoughts with negativity. Continue to motivate and pour that aspiration in your heart, to keep it alive until you succeed. When your passion is strong and unwavering, you never give up easily nor feel too tired to chase your dreams. As you keep going, you'll feel the infusion of joy, happiness and the type of inner satisfaction that fuels your energy with the power of pure love.

It's very important to be optimistic and have positive people around you, people that give you good energy and feedback. Because once you start mingling with negative people, you can easily become negative too. Negative people often don't see the precious and brilliant side of your dreams and they're prone to putting other people down and criticising their dreams. Or if you're with people who always complain, you realise that one day you start complaining too. Negative people always see the negative side of life and it stops them moving forward. People who always complain are everywhere and they become hard to always be around. They always complain, they complain about everything and it can drain your positive energy. So, keep holding your dreams in high regard because it's only you who knows how to keep them brightly shining.

Try to stay clear of the constant complainer. Of course, I don't mean that you physically push them away, but try to not let their negativity impact your life and your decisions.

Just look at it as a lesson. You can think, 'oh, this poor lady needs some help. She has so much negativity in herself that she can't see the bright side of life. She is so full of negativity that she hasn't got any room for positivity.'

It's important to our wellbeing to stay positive, to stay connected with positive good people, people who share the same vision and dream.

Some people are always happy, they radiate joy

wherever they are and whatever they do. They're filled with positive energy and they always keep reenergising that positive energy in every encounter. They spread joy simply through being themselves.

It is my dream to share my experience with people in the hope that I may impact one or two people in a positive way. And if one person that I impact can impact another person then it creates a ripple effect.

I want to share with women and young generations that life is beautiful, that they just need to keep dreaming and not to give up easily.

And when people's talents and skills are being nurtured and enhanced, they naturally contribute better to society and fulfil themselves in the process. It's a cycle of positivity.

Inventor Thomas Edison said, "If we did all the things we were capable of, we would literally astound ourselves."

I believe this is true. When given the right chance, right place and right people around you, we can all literally astound ourselves.

"When we ACCEPT it allows us to DECIDE to move forward and DREAM endlessly."
— Sarifa Alonto-Younes

⪦ MY DREAMS ⪧

Write down your dreams. Your small dreams and your big dreams. Remember: dreaming is free!

....

....

....

....

....

....

....

....

....

....

....

....

....

....

....

....

....

....

....

> *" The biggest adventure you can take is to live the life of your dreams. "*
> **Oprah Winfrey**

CHAPTER SEVEN

GROW TALL

There comes a time when people reach a new level, it's another hierarchy of success, which I call Grow TALL.

Once you have reached a certain level of development, for example maybe you have a good education, or have fulfilled your dreams, or maybe you're an entrepreneur or in the management or leadership sector.

Some people choose to never reach this level, they are satisfied with their current state and that is fine. But often, once we have reached a certain level of competence or achievement we want to give back to others or develop in new ways.

This new level that I call 'Grow TALL' has new ways to innovate, achieve, grow and learn. And like any new level of accomplishment it comes complete with its own series of obstacles and challenges.

Grow TALL is ideal for people with big dreams, people who wish to go to a new level and impact their communities, cities and continents on a grander scale. They can typically be teachers, leaders, entrepreneurs, political leaders, managers, mothers, caretakers and community-driven influencers.

Many times they have staff or teams or people to co-ordinate and integrate.

Grow TALL is a hierarchy of reaching the next stage of your development but it helps as a guide for how to interact with others, or nurture staff or grow a like-minded community.

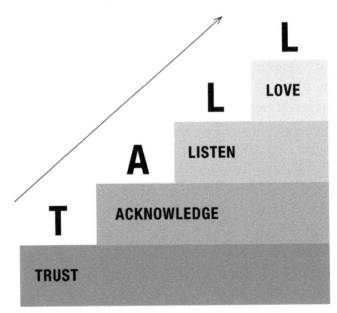

TRUST

Trust is crucial to growth. You need to trust yourself and trust your abilities. You also need to trust the people around you.

You need to trust the people working with you or for you. Trust that they are the right people to contribute and that they'll do the right thing for you or for the organisation.

We have often been taught to not trust others. To be suspicious of them and look for hidden agendas. However, we must remember that people want to feel good about themselves, they want to progress and develop and they want to fulfil their goals too.

Recent surveys showed that workers from all over the world said that a high level of trust in their employer would influence them to be happier in their job, stay committed to the company and be more engaged and productive.[4]

And furthermore, they even outlined which factors would help promote trust.

The main aspects nominated as "very important" to the majority of global workers were:

- The employer "Delivers on promises" — 67%
- The employer "Provides job security" — 64%
- The employer "Provides fair compensation and good benefits" — 63%
- The employer "Communicates openly/ transparently" — 59%
- The employer "provides equal opportunity for pay and promotion for all people regardless of differences" and "operates ethically" — both 57%.

---

4 https://www.ey.com/gl/en/about-us/our-people-and-culture/
ey-global-study-trust-in-the-workplace

Trust is built when it is given. By being ethical and honourable and fair to your team and fellow workers, trust grows and grows.

Even workers who work remotely are to be given trust. You do not need to micro-manage every person if your systems are built correctly. In fact, statistics show that people who work away from the office (such as in their own home or on the road) actually overcompensate with their communication and work longer hours to show their colleagues and boss that they are in fact working.

> *"The best way to find out if you can trust*
> *somebody is to trust them."*
> **Ernest Hemingway**

ACKNOWLEDGE

Acknowledge others. Acknowledge whatever talents, weaknesses, strengths and contributions they may have, or have made, because that's what helps organisations and groups grow, and continue to grow.

When you understand the weaknesses, that's where you can prepare and train them, provide them with professional development and training. This gives them strength and helps them feel good about themselves. Acknowledge their strengths and weaknesses, without making anyone feel wrong or bad. By acknowledging others, you validate their contribution.

A research study in 2013 by Globoforce revealed

that 89% of people are more motivated by being told what they're doing right than by being told what they're doing wrong. It also showed that around 80% looked for this recognition to be offered near the time of the activity they were doing, or very soon after.

Employee-recognition expert and bestselling author Bob Nelson noticed similar tendencies when it came to recognition. One of the studies he conducted with 598 employees who reported to managers showed that around 77.6 percent said that it was very or extremely important to be recognised by their managers when they do good work. That is a high percentage and it's reflective of the general working population.

The study showed that employees expected recognition to occur: immediately (20 percent), soon thereafter (52.9 percent), or sometime later (18.8 percent).

He believes, "You get what you reward."

From my experience with team members, I believe acknowledgement is the antidote to resentment or feeling used. It reminds people that you really do value and appreciate them.

A recent management study from Robert Half revealed that 46% of employees leave a company because they feel underappreciated. A whopping 61% said their bosses don't place much importance on them as people, and 88% said they do not receive adequate acknowledgement for the work they do.

Acknowledgement doesn't take a lot of time, mere seconds in fact, but its impacts are far-reaching.

Simon Sinek said, "Leaders don't look for recognition from others, leaders look for others to recognize."

"Of all the skills of leadership, listening is the most valuable — and one of the least understood. Most captains of industry listen only sometimes, and they remain ordinary leaders. But a few, the great ones, never stop listening. That's how they get word before anyone else of unseen problems and opportunities."
Peter Nulty, Fortune Magazine

LISTEN

Not listening to others, not giving them space to express themselves and their ideas openly can actually stunt them, make them hide and become afraid. According to a recent study, more than 40 percent of junior-level workers state that they are afraid to bring ideas or concerns to upper management.

As the former CEO of the Sarah Lee Corporation, John Bryan once said, "You have to be willing sometimes to listen to some remarkable bad opinions. Because if you say to someone, 'That's the silliest thing I've ever heard; get on out of here!' — then you'll never get anything out of that person again, and you might as well have a puppet on a string or a robot."

Your staff are your team. They see things that others don't. They are often 'in the trenches' of the business and understand what is working and what isn't.

They are your eyes and ears. By listening to them it helps the organisation grow and keep growing, because they are also your brain, the brain of the organisation and they're an asset. Listening to others accelerates the progress of any relationship, team or organisation.

Interestingly, 34% of employees worldwide think that their company doesn't listen to their ideas for improving the business. And a huge 82% of employees have ideas about how their company can achieve better performance. Imagine the difference listening could make to future business leaders.

Listening is caring. Listening is an act of love.

"The biggest communication problem is we do not listen to understand. We listen to reply."
Stephen R. Covey

LOVE

Then comes love. Love is life's medicine to everything. It's important to love people. To be a channel and provider of love. Everybody needs love. Regardless of, whether you're at home with your family, or at work with your colleagues, or with your friends, everybody needs to be loved. It's one of our deepest and most vital human needs.

And loving people helps them grow. If you have staff, remember that they are giving their loyalty to the company. So it's important to nurture them, motivate them and provide them with the necessary skills and knowledge they need; and then they will never leave you because they have everything they could possibly want and need.

When you have fulfilled that potential, the organisation, *your* organisation will only keep growing and your staff members will be happy. If you look after them right, what would they look for outside?

Staff members leave when they're not happy. When they're not getting that trust or acknowledgement. When they're not being listened to or they're not being loved. Even a child cannot grow without love.

A Gallup study of 7,272 U.S. adults revealed that one in two had left their job to get away from their manager or boss so they could improve their overall life. That's a big statistic.

"Love" may not be the first word you think of when thinking about business or your workplace but it has a strong influence on our personal levels of satisfaction. Of course, I'm not talking about romantic love but genuine caring love.

Researchers Sigal Barsade from the Joseph Frank Bernstein Professor of Management at Wharton and Olivia A. O'Neill, an Associate Professor of Management at George Mason University and Senior Scientist at the Center for the Advancement of Well-Being discovered that love in the workplace does matter. In fact, it matters a whole lot.

The study called "What's Love Got to Do With It?: The Influence of a Culture of Companionate Love in the Long-term Care Setting" showed that employees who felt they worked in a loving, caring culture reported higher levels of satisfaction and teamwork. They showed up to work more often.

Another follow-up study that included 3,201 employees from seven different industries reflected a similar result. People who worked in a place where they felt free to express care, affection, and compassion for each other were more satisfied with their jobs, more committed to the company, and more accountable for their performance.

So this culture of love is vital. Managers and organisations can provide this love, they can create warm and safe environments for their employees and ensure they promote a culture of care and inclusiveness. Imagine if workplaces were full of support and positive energy for all.

So, I believe that love conquers everything. And for me that's the very foundation of everything, to love. Love enables you to reach self-actualization.

"We are made for loving. If we don't love,
we will be like plants without water."
Desmond Tutu

+++

"Without TRUST nothing starts,
without LOVE everything ends."
Sarifa Alonto-Younes

WAYS I CAN "GROW TALL"

TRUST

ACKNOWLEDGE

_____

_____

_____

_____

_____

_____

_____

_____

_____

_____

_____

_____

LISTEN

_____

_____

_____

_____

_____

_____

_____

_____

_____

_____

....

....

....

....

....

LOVE ....

....

....

....

....

....

....

....

....

....

....

....

....

....

....

....

....

CHAPTER EIGHT

SELF-ACTUALISATION:
THE REAL SUCCESS IN LIFE

The ultimate goal is to 'know thyself'. To be self-actualised.

The first hierarchy of success is to — Accept, Decide and Dream.

The second hierarchy of success is to Grow TALL.

The ultimate hierarchy of success is self-actualisation.

And once you reach self-actualisation, you will be the most successful person on earth. And that self-actualisation is very hard to reach because some people may stay only in the primary hierarchy of success, which is to accept, decide and dream and they're happy.

That's fine. But if you want to grow further, if you're in a management position or an entrepreneur or leader, you need to Grow TALL to reach self-actualisation.

As Abraham Maslow illustrated through his

"Hierarchy of Needs" but which I refer to as the "Hierarchy of Success," Maslow believed that real human motivation is based on an individual's ability to seek fulfillment and change through personal growth and development.

Maslow believed that individuals strive for higher needs when their lower-level needs have been satisfied. And this idea also enables us to think of the whole of society, to lift others out of their lower-level needs so they can fulfil their potential and contribute to the greater good of society.

Women, for example, we need to equip ourselves as a whole with the necessary skills and knowledge if we want to lift up each other, contribute to society and make a global difference.

Looking at the lowest-level needs and simply meeting these as a global community should be a priority. Providing nutritious food, clean water and adequate shelter for all citizens is imperative to our success as a society.

Maslow's Hierachy of Needs

Maslow's Hierachy of Needs

Level 1 needs are the physiological human needs like food, water, air, and sleep. The basics in life.

Level 2 needs are those of safety and security, often the type of dangers that arises from social, employment or political instability.

Level 3 needs are those of love and a sense of belonging and connectedness.

Level 4 needs are those of for self-confidence and a healthy self-esteem.

Level 5 is the deeper need for self-actualisation. This is the summit of all human needs because we all want to reach a level of self-mastery, a level that reflects and embodies our full potential and allows us to express it authentically. This gives us true satisfaction and fulfilment.

Characteristics of Self-Actualising People

Maslow studied 18 people that he considered to be self-actualised. He identified 15 specific characteristics of a self-actualised person. He studied people like Albert Einstein, Abraham Lincoln, Martin Luther King Jr., Helen Keller, Mahatma Gandhi and Thomas Jefferson.

1. *Efficient perceptions of reality*

Self-actualisers perceive reality accurately and can judge situations with clarity and honesty. They are very aware and sensitive to false and dishonest people and situations. They are independent and not reliant on other people or their environment to form opinions and views.

2. *Comfortable acceptance of self, others and nature*

They accept themselves and others for what they are.

3. *Spontaneous and natural*

True to oneself, rather than being how others want. They do not allow rules and regulations to stop them from achieving their mission if they believe such rules are incorrect or trivial. They do have strong ethics but their ideas do not always correspond with that of society.

4. *Task-centered*

Self-actualisers have a mission to fulfil some task or problem 'beyond' themselves. They often see their work as a calling.

5. *Humour*

They have the ability to laugh at themselves (but do not enjoy jokes at other people's expense).

6. *Able to look at life objectively*

Self-actualisers can assess life and its interwoven relationships with a clear objectivity, they do not view life through a false or superficial lens.

7. *Creative*

Self-actualisers possess a unique creativity, originality or ingenuity in their field.

8. *Independent*

Self-actualisers are independent thinkers rather than blind followers of society's rules. They do not deliberately rebel against authority or resist convention, but will do if it's important to them. They would rather operate from within the system to bring about reform than to launch attacks from the outside. Self-actualisers are free from reliance on external authorities or other people but instead are resourceful and independent.

9. *Humanitarian*

Self-actualisers are socially compassionate and possess a love and concern for humanity.

10. *Appreciate life*

They possess a deep appreciation for basic life-experiences. The self-actualiser seems to appreciate life's natural goodness — they maintain an awe-like, fresh wonder about 'small things' — a sunset or a flower can be experienced as if it were the first time.

11. Profound interpersonal relationships

They establish deep, loving and satisfying interpersonal relationships with a few people. They usually have few closer intimate friends than a large number of superficial relationships.

12. Peak experiences

Self-actualisers report frequent moments of peak experiences, these occasions were often marked by intense feelings of harmony, oneness and deep meaning. Self-actualisers reported feeling at one with the universe, filled with light, beauty, goodness and divinity.

13. Comfortable with solitude

Despite their profound relationships with others, self-actualising people are comfortable being alone and deeply value moments of solitude.

14. Democratic

Self-actualisers are democratic. They do not discriminate on grounds of class, qualifications, beliefs, orientation, culture, gender, age race or colour. They are open and willing to learn from anyone who is their superior in a given field.

15. Strong moral/ethical standards

Self-actualisers usually have a strong inner code of ethics and a moral compass between right and wrong. While they do not usually preach religion in the orthodox sense, they do have high standards of human behaviour.

To become self-actualised is the ultimate success, it aligns all parts of you and amplifies your skills, decisions, values, purpose and dreams all in the same seamless direction. It means you can authentically be who you were destined to be.

Future Leaders — You Can Become One

We know that the world thrives with good leadership. But this leadership must be balanced and reflect the best of humanity. It's my dream to help create some of the world's future leaders, to give them the internal and external tools they need to succeed.

Even in a country as open-minded as Australia, only 13.7% of chair positions are women, 25.8% are directors and only 17.1% are CEOs. 30.5% of women hold key management personnel positions.[5]

This is because women can't equally compete with our male counterparts as many of the male-dominated systems and industries are internally imbalanced.

Women worldwide require empowerment. And the best way to empower a woman is through education. When women are educated, it means that we are informed and have a greater scope of understanding. Our abilities get enhanced and then we can dream, and dream with all our will, might and power.

If you look at Third World countries, they are lagging behind economically and in progress and development, and perhaps it's not a coincidence because women in general are not educated and empowered in many countries.

---

5   WGEA (2019), WGEA Data Explorer, <data.wgea.gov.au>

Women cannot fully contribute to the progress of the country if they're not given the right education or skills to do so. Globally we don't have enough women in the workforce and that is because of education. Men are often given more educational opportunities and therefore more working opportunities.

In 18 countries, husbands can legally prevent their wives from working. This type of suppression does not help us become a fair, just and thriving society.

And if you look at countries that are thriving, they advance because men and women are working hand in hand, shoulder to shoulder to perform jobs accordingly. Jobs should not be designated as this 'for men' and that 'for women'. There are plenty of jobs that both men and women can do.

The European Union conducted a study revealing that by 2050, gender equality would produce an increase of two-and-a-half trillion euros and increase the number of jobs by over 10 million.[6] Though these figures sound wonderful, we need gender equality first. And to get that we must provide women and girls with equality, education and opportunity.

According to UNESCO less than 40% of countries provide girls and boys with equal access to education. And only 39% of countries have equal proportions of boys and girls enrolled in secondary education. On top

---

6 "Economic Benefits of Gender Equality in the European Union," European Institute for Gender Equality, https://eige.europa.eu/gender-mainstreaming/policy-areas/economic-and-financial-affairs/economic-benefits-gender-equality

of that, there are 774 million illiterate adults in the world today and two-thirds of those are women.

What is also surprising is the sad fact that the proportion of illiterate women has not changed for the last 20 years. What is also confronting is the numbers of our illiterate youth, they account for 123 million and 76 million are female.

Being illiterate creates big limitations. Even if people work in a job, they can't meet the highest standard in that job if they don't have a proper education in how to do it. How we can advance as a society if we don't reach out and help those in need?

According to the United Nations, over 265 million children are currently out of school and 22% of them are of primary school age. There are also 617 million youth worldwide that lack basic mathematics and literacy skills. What happens to those 617 million children? What future do they have? How many limitations will they face during their lives?

Prejudice against girls is still prevalent in our education systems and I am here to help change that. Although women have actually overtaken men in the number of them obtaining a higher education globally, in many many countries the epidemic of gender inequality remains rampant.

In today's modern society, women remain underrepresented in scientific and technological areas, only 29% of the world's researchers are women. Many face social and cultural barriers to obtaining leadership and management positions.

In the agriculture sector only 13 percent of women are agricultural land holders. In fact, in 39 countries, daughters and sons do not have equal inheritance rights and 49 countries lack laws to protect women from domestic violence. As you can see, there's much work to do.

But the good news is, if we educate girls and women, we change the world. We really do.

Educated mothers have healthier children. A child born to a mother who can read is 50% more likely to survive past the age of 5.[7] Each extra year of a mother's schooling reduces the probability of infant mortality by 5% — 10%.[8]

An educated female population increases a country's productivity and fuels economic growth. Some countries lose more than $1 billion a year by failing to educate girls to the same level as boys.[9]

Gandhi said, "the future is with woman."

We must believe this too and dream for a better future. A dream that equips other women and girls with equality, opportunity and education. We need to help women and the younger generations, we need to close that gap because if children are not educated and empowered it stunts the growth of the individual and the world.

---

7 http://www.education-transforms.org/en/?portfolio=test-2-2-educating-girls-can-save-millions-of-lives#.UxSs-fldWSo

8 http://www.education-transforms.org/en/?portfolio=test-a-matter-of-life-and-death#.UxSoGPldWSo

9 https://plan-international.org/publications?lang=fr

Many great leaders are active in this arena and I believe we are building a new era of conscious leadership in some sectors.

Michelle Obama is one such leader. Of course, best-known for her role as the first lady of the United States but what many don't know is that throughout her life, Michelle faced a host of challenges and met them head-on.

During her time as the first lady, she made a significant and lasting impact on social issues in the US. Though she was sometimes met with hostility, she rose above it and continued to work toward her goals.

She also achieved amazing things outside of her role as the first lady. Since the end of her husband's second term, she has worked relentlessly to support important causes. Her memoir, *Becoming*, was one of the fastest-selling nonfiction books in history.

For those who haven't read it, here's a small snapshot of a blog I wrote about her and some areas where she overcame obstacles and inspired others.

+++

Young Michelle Robinson attended a high school for gifted children. She was a star student with a lot of drive and ambition. Michelle often said that her parents' support contributed to her success and confidence

Unfortunately, like many, she ran into prejudice at a young age. Some of her teachers were sceptical of her ability to succeed. But Michelle wasn't daunted.

If anything, this strengthened her determination.

Like her older brother, she attended Princeton and pursued a bachelor's degree in sociology and graduated summa cum laude. She became one of the few African-American women in her generation to attend Harvard Law School and graduated in 1988, but not before she took part in protests calling for more diversity in her program.

Michelle started her career as an associate in a big-name Chicago law firm. Her areas of expertise were property law and marketing.

It was here she met Barack Obama. In the summer of 1989, he interned at the firm and she was his advisor. At first, she was hesitant to enter a romantic relationship with someone she worked with. But they eventually started going out and discovered they had a lot in common. The couple married in 1992.

Since a profession in law didn't turn out as fulfilling as she had hoped for, she switched over to public service. For a while, she worked as an assistant to the Mayor of Chicago.

In 1993, Michelle Obama became the executive director for the Chicago branch of Public Allies.

This non-profit organisation helps develop young people's leadership skills with a focus on minority groups. In her memoir, Michelle mentioned that this was her favourite job.

Helping children and young adults became a priority for her. She started to work with universities in Chicago to improve student services and community relations.

As she gained one prestigious position after another, she also became a mother. Malia Obama was born in 1998 and Sasha in 2001.

After Barack Obama came out of nowhere to win the presidency in 2008, the family moved into the White House. Michelle was full of her own plans.

One of the best-known decisions she made as first lady was growing a vegetable garden around the White House. This brought public attention to healthy food choices and childhood obesity. She covered her views on nutrition in her first book, *American Grown*.

Other issues of interest to Michelle Obama include education and sports in disadvantaged communities. She often spoke of the importance of community service and taking initiative.

In early 2017, the Obamas moved out of the White House. Michelle Obama continued her dedication to promoting health and equality.

She has taught many people how to change things for the better.

+++

What are the lessons we can learn from Michelle Obama's story? It's good to ask this because we can all learn from each other. And of course, it's not only Michelle Obama's story, there are many women that belong to minority groups and they too teach us similar lessons.

Here are some lessons I feel are important.

Lesson #1 — Build Your Personal Brand

When Michelle Obama joined her husband on the campaign trail in 2008, she left a great impression on the public. Her speeches were articulate, passionate and moving, and she spoke bravely and candidly about social issues.

She is decisive, determined and fearless in the pursuit of what matters to her. The way she presents herself to the world is part of her message. Everything from her rhetorical skills to her fashion choices serves her goals.

In other words, Michelle Obama's personal brand reflects her philosophy.

She also makes use of her unique experiences to build her arguments. When speaking to young people, she is careful to bring their attention to the opportunities that lie ahead. She also speaks about the difficulties, including some of the obstacles that she ran into.

Being open about her own life isn't new to her. But writing a memoir was still challenging, as it was more intimate than her public speeches.

She rose to the occasion and wrote about some sensitive personal topics. For example, she wrote about the fertility issues she had to deal with before conceiving.

One of the aims of her book was to give women a sense of hope and motivation. The memoir's reception proved that she achieved this.

What is your personal brand?

What is your life philosophy and how do you best represent this to others?

Lesson #2 – Speak Up About Your Needs and Follow Your Principles

As a mother of two, Michelle Obama seeks a careful work-life balance.

At one point, she even took one of her infant daughters to a job interview. In part, this was a practical solution to a problem — she couldn't find anyone to babysit on short notice. But it was also a deliberate decision, as she wanted to make it clear that her family life was important to her.

Here is how she remembers this moment:

"Sasha was a fact of my life. *Here is me*, I was saying, *and here also is my baby*."

This kind of integrity and sincerity followed Michelle throughout her career. It helped her weather the obstacles of being under constant scrutiny as a public figure.

* What are your principles?
* What matters most to you?

Lesson #3 – Don't Let Anyone Tell You That You Can't

Near the end of her high school education, one of her teachers told her that she "wasn't Princeton material".

This could have been a huge blow to her confidence. But instead of taking it to heart, she decided to prove the naysayer wrong.

It wasn't the first or last time that someone told her she couldn't reach her goals. At times, she was also faced with open animosity and mockery.

During his first presidential election campaign, the political landscape in the US was increasingly fraught, and that meant that there was no room for error.

In spite of their perseverance, Michelle Obama was ready for the possibility that Barack would lose the election. But she wasn't going to let that stop her own campaigning efforts.

After the victory, she became even more determined to help her family weather all the pressure they faced. Through her work as first lady, she gained admirers from across the political spectrum.

Nobody would ever underestimate her again. In fact, some expected her to run for president in 2020, though she never expressed any such wishes.

She said, "One of the lessons that I grew up with was to always stay true to yourself and never let what somebody else says distract you from your goals."

How can you keep moving on with your goals and dreams despite obstacles or what other people may say?

Lesson #4 – Follow Your Passion

Most of Michelle Obama's professional life focuses on the things she really cares about.

Passion drives her causes and helps her inspire others.

It's important to follow your passion with quiet

strength and stay true to yourself.

* What are you passionate about?

"I am an example of what is possible when girls from the very beginning of their lives are loved and nurtured by people around them. I was surrounded by extraordinary women in my life who taught me about quiet strength and dignity."
— **Michelle Obama**

Lesson #5 – Public Speaking and the Power of One

During her time as the first lady, Michelle Obama's speeches were just as inspiring as her husband's. She always had an imposing presence as a public figure. But it was far more stressful to speak when the eyes of the world were on her. She handled this incredible pressure with grace. She had a dedicated team that helped her find the best ways to cover all her talking points.

She listened to the experts who helped make her speeches perfect. She also practiced the speeches extensively. Every single detail got planned out in advance, and this helped her find her confidence and allow for natural spontaneity too.

During her book tour, the people who attended enjoyed her natural charisma and spontaneity.

Michelle Obama knew that one person could make a massive difference. That one speech, one person and one dream was often all one needed to change

the landscape of possibility. Her ability to keep this in mind at all times proved that she was grounded and authentic. She said, "You may not always have a comfortable life and you will not always be able to solve all of the world's problems at once but don't ever underestimate the importance you can have because history has shown us that courage can be contagious and hope can take on a life of its own."
 * *Where can you make a difference?*
 * *Do your words reflect you and empower others?*

Lesson #6 — Be Willing to Change Course and Use Obstacles as Opportunities

The exact course of Michelle Obama's life was impossible to predict. There were many times when she had to stop and reconsider her goals. She forged her own path and found new opportunities.

This flexibility is a critical factor in her success as well as her ability to use obstacles to her advantage, to forge a new way forward, not only for herself but for others too.

"You should never view your challenges as a disadvantage. Instead, it's important for you to understand that your experience facing and overcoming adversity is actually one of your biggest advantage."
Michelle Obama

Michelle Obama is of course a prominent figure and her leadership qualities also exist in women all over the globe. When she said, "you should never view your challenges as a disadvantage," she spoke a universal language to all minority groups or disadvantaged citizens.

The famous incident on December 1, 1955, when Rosa Parks refused to give up her bus seat to a white passenger spoke a universal language too. It was a quiet and remarkable act of defiance that helped ignite the Civil Rights Movement. But this now famous act wasn't the only remarkable thing about Rosa Parks.

At age 16 Rosa dropped out of school to take care of her dying grandmother. When she was 19 years old, she returned to school to complete her high school education. She went on to receive her diploma in 1933, at the time this made her part of only seven percent of African Americans to earn the distinction. She went on to receive more than forty-three honorary doctorate degrees, write many books, meet Presidents and religious figures and was voted by *Time Magazine* one of The 100 Most Influential People of the 20th Century.

Because when we stand for our self, we also stand for others.

My personal stance isn't only mine, it's for all women and young girls, all minority groups, all people. And I beg that yours be the same. We need more empowerment, unity and acceptance in this world. Begin within.

"Achievements and success can only be meaningful when they make a significant difference and change a soul for the betterment of humanity and society."
Sarifa Alonto-Younes

CHAPTER NINE

THE VISION

Now that you have heard my story, the adversity and obstacles, the success and failures, you can see it was a journey of many ups and downs. I had to face and outgrow my former self.

I have shared my story many times and will continue to do so, both on stage speaking and through my writing. It's my calling. Not because of me. It's not about me. I don't share my story to boast or earn sympathy or recognition. I share it for the sake of those who are ready to hear it and for those struggling to overcome their obstacles in the hope it may help them turn obstacles into opportunities and advantages. And, likewise I wish to invite you to share your insights, your story and your journey of embracing and loving your obstacles, so you too may inspire others to do the same.

You see, real change has always come from a few individuals who pursued their vision and mission to achieve their dreams with unwavering commitment. They then inspired some and those in turn, inspired others and so on. As Margaret Mead, anthropologist and recipient of the Planetary Citizen of the Year Award in 1978 said, "Never doubt that a small group of thoughtful, committed citizens can change the world: indeed, it's the only thing that ever has."

You may think that your story is different and not worth sharing. Wrong! Every story is worth sharing, and every story holds insight for someone. For those that hear your story it might hold the key to improve, enhance or change their life for the better.

So, share your story, be the impact in the world that helps bring about the changes you want to see. My invitation to you is this — share your story, share my story, send people my website or the book website or amazon link, tell people about me, my message, this book, speak about what you got from it for you and how it impacted you.

Then, identify your mission or calling, your 'why' and follow it fully.

Share your story of overcoming adversity, of loving your obstacles and inspire others to do so — help others be better versions of themselves to help humanity rise up to its fullest potential. We owe it to our ancestors and our children and their children's children. Thank you for reading this book, for sharing it, for living it and sharing your story.

Sarifa Alonto-Younes

⤝ MY STORY MATTERS ⤞

Be brave and write a small chapter about *you*.
What's your unique story? Have you had an obstacle and turned it into an opportunity? If you feel really brave, you can also share your story with me at sarifayounes.com

*Let us remember:
One book, one pen,
one child, and
one teacher can
change the world.*
Malala Yousafzai

ABOUT THE AUTHOR

Sarifa Alonto-Younes was born in the Alonto family of the Philippines. She was born in Marawi City from the Maranao of the Lake Lanao of the Philippines in January 3, 1971. She is the proud daughter of late father, Regaro Alonto (from Ramain Ditsaan and Maul Marantao) and late mother, Magalao Arumponi (from Ramain Ditsaan).

Her father passed away when she was three years old and only a few years later, her mother lost her battle with cancer. When her mother passed away she was brought up by her uncle and aunty (Minodar Dimaampao and Limpaco Dimnang) who looked after her and loved her and lived with Dumarpa and Sarah Macarambon's family. Sarah stood as a mother, sister and a friend to Sarifa together with her seven children and they all grew up together like siblings under one roof.

Struggling to see the beauty and light in the world, and recognising that the local scope for a woman in her culture was limited, she knew the only way out was through education. Wanting to help not only herself but those countless young children and women disadvantaged by their circumstances, or with little scope to move beyond the roles and career opportunities that tradition dictated, Sarifa put her heart and soul into her studies. Thus, a doorway for her future life journey.

Sarifa was determined not only change her life, but those of others too; she was driven to earn top marks, scholarships and ultimately the opportunity to study overseas. Little did she know that her pursuit would not only make a difference to her hometown, but far beyond.

Fast forward, and within three decades and Sarifa is inspiring generations of young students through her schools, service and story every day.

Her passion for education saw Sarifa and her husband Hassan found and build a preschool in Melbourne Australia, the Arndell Park Early Childhood Learning Centre, found and build an international school in Philippines, the International academy of Marawi (I AM) and go on to also found and build the Training College of Australia (RTO) which provide countless students with vocational training and qualification courses.

She also established and owned three travel agencies

between 2006-2017.

Sarifa has spoken at global events and summits, been interviewed on national and international media such as newspapers, magazines, television and radio in Malaysia, Turkey, the Philippines, Australia and a number of countries across Europe on education, environmental and gender equality centred topics.

Sarifa is widely published across magazines, newspapers, online news, environmental and educational publications and is frequently sought out by media for commentary. In 1994 she was awarded by her university, IIUM, as the most Active Student Leader.

Her passion and commitment has seen her inspire students to collaborate and deliver their environmental research and solutions at the Global Youth Summit four years running. She's also the winner of the Australian award in 2018, AusMumpreneur for Multicultural Business Excellence Award and a finalist of the 2019 AusMumpreneur, Women Will Change the World Award category. She is also the Chairperson for the Melbourne chapter of HerStory Women's Global Empowerment Conference.

Trained in psychology, Sarifa has worked with women, children, teens and the elderly in all areas, from mental health wards to being a school counsellor.

She has ventured a number of successful businesses, yet the greatest reward does not come from profit-and-loss statements, but from positively impacting more lives.

Sarifa tirelessly works to improve the scope for women globally, particularly in Third World countries. She has been helping orphans, poor families, the elderly and disadvantaged since 2008 and believes that lifting up disadvantaged children's lives through education will eradicate poverty and violence.

Sarifa works long hours across multiple projects and speaks internationally to audiences on education, political and environmental issues, women's empowerment and social issues. It is this book, her keynote presentations and her unwavering commitment to opening up equal opportunities for people of all walks of life that fuels her drive every day.

Most importantly, Sarifa is a devoted mother to four beautiful children, Adam, Nahda, Ahmad and Dania and faithful, dedicated wife to her loving, caring and supportive husband, Hassan.

She has come a long long way from the days of being a hurt and disadvantaged orphan back in the Philippines. Yet without this beginning she would not be standing here today asking the world to love their own obstacles.

Her love for humanity, equality and education is a gift for all.

Sarifa's next book will further explore the Grow TALL principles.

To stay up-to-date with Sarifa's next book and speaking events go to: **www.sarifayounes.com** or email: info@sarifayounes.com or sarifa@arndell-park.com.au

ACKNOWLEDGEMENTS

In memory of my late parents and loved ones who contributed directly or indirectly to my success.

My loving, caring and supportive husband, Hassan, who is always there to give life to my dreams and endeavours without any hesitation.

To my children, Adam, Nahda, Ahmad and Dania, who are my inspiration as I watch them grow. Their pure love fuels my energy to keep going.

My late Babu Hadja Naima and Bapa Hadji Ali for stepping in and filling the gap when I lost my father and then my mother.

My thanks and gratitude to late Dumarpa Sr. and Sarah Macarambon and their children whom I grew up with together under one roof after the death of my mother. Thank you all for your love and care through the years that I needed you most.

Late Engr, Mangolamba and children for the love and guidance you have always provided, even after my marriage you were always there for me, my husband

and our whole family.

My relatives, cousins, sisters and lifetime friends; Hamida, Murshida, Mufaida and Rossmia who had been my inspirations and companions from when we were in Malaysia together. We have shared a lot of memories, experiences and laughter of which I'll treasure forever.

To late kuya Maya (Ismayatin Ibrahim) and our foster father, Dr. Ahmad Hassoubah, for their valuable advice, guidance and help when I was in Malaysia.

My siblings, families and relatives in the Philippines and in-laws in Lebanon who are always there for me in good times and bad times. Too many of you to name. Thank you.

My late father-in-law and late mother-in-law who both showered me with love, understanding and compassion.

My brothers-in-law and their wives and my one and only sister-in-law who are always beside us to cheer and show support to our journey.

To Raisalam, you are incredibly amazing and I can't thank you enough for your love and support.

To Erik Bigalk who put a seed in my head that I should write a book, I am thankful and grateful to you.

I would like also to acknowledge the Speakers Institute CEO and Founder Sam Cawthorn, Kate Cawthorn, Warren Tate, Catherine Molloy and all the Speakers Institute members for encouraging me to keep growing and to lean in within the proximity as the "Best Is Yet To Come".

My thanks to Peace Mitchell and Katy Garner of

AusMumpreneur for supporting, recognising and empowering Australian women business entrepreneurs, including me, to make a difference for the betterment of humanity and society.

I would like to express my gratitude and appreciation to the CEO of Dean Publishing, Ms. Susan Dean, who supports me as an author, a woman and business entrepreneur. Natalie Deane, chief editor, who helped bring my story to life in a truly authentic way. Jazmine Morales, for her incredible design. Thank you to Monique, Chloe, Michael and the team. Without Dean Publishing's untiring efforts and encouragement, this book would not have been possible. With their sincere and incredible support, they have brought this dream from a concept to reality.

Those people who had impacted my life forever, you know who you are. You are always in my heart and I am grateful and thankful to all of you.

"A hero is an ordinary individual who finds the strength to persevere and endure in spite of overwhelming obstacles."
Christopher Reeve

SARIFA'S KEYNOTE PRESENTATIONS

Love Your Obstacles –
How to turn challenges into opportunities

Imagine how many people are going through different types of obstacles every day. There is a global struggle to cope with various forms of obstacles in our lives, they could range from illiteracy, loss of jobs or loved ones, incidents or accidents that may have devastating effects on physical, mental, emotional, relationships, work or even business operations for those who have businesses. For some people, obstacles can break them and spin them into cycle of hardship and depression. For others, obstacles can define and strengthen them beyond their wildest imagination.

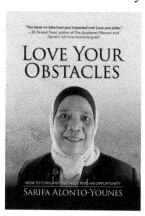

Sarifa discovered a secret formula that will help transform individuals thinking and many lives forever. Sarifa's inspiring story of struggle and triumph will help anyone face and overcome obstacles in life with a new sense of passion, purpose and grace.

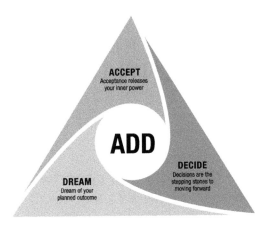

Never has there been a better time to learn how to *Love Your Obstacles*. Achievements and success can only be meaningful when they make a difference and change a soul for the betterment of humanity and society.

In this keynote, you will learn Sarifa's 'Accept, Decide and Dream' formula so you can achieve and live the life of your dreams.

The Hierarchy of Success –
How to Help Your Organisation Grow TALL

Every business owner, manager or organisations' ultimate goal is to keep the business or organisation financially healthy and sound. Likewise, its human power like employees or staff members that are the key assets to the organisation. Therefore, it's important that all team members must resonate and align with the vision and mission of the organisation to fuel economic growth and achieve continuous success.

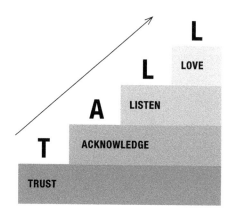

Sarifa will engage you and your team to help understand the needs of healthy businesses and organisations in relation to the behaviour of the staff members or employees. Every business or organisation needs to grow TALL so it can continuously grow and sustain itself.

In this session, you will discover the Grow TALL principles:

- T – When and how to TRUST
- A – The power of ACKNOWLEDGEMENT
- L – The secret and art of LISTENING
- L – The influence of LOVE

≤ NOTES ≥

"Without TRUST nothing starts,
without LOVE everything ends."
Sarifa Alonto-Younes

Contact Sarifa
www.sarifayounes.com
info@sarifayounes.com